MARIE
CURIE

MOLLIE
KELLER

MARIE CURIE

FRANKLIN WATTS
NEW YORK | LONDON | TORONTO | SYDNEY | 1982
AN IMPACT BIOGRAPHY

FOR
JENNIFER AND ABIGAIL,
AND
ESPECIALLY FOR DAVID

Cover photograph courtesy of Culver Pictures

Photographs courtesy of: Culver Pictures Inc.: pp. 10, 15, 24, 43, 69, 74; American Institute of Physics Neils Bohr Library, William G. Myers Collection: pp. 60, 111; United Press International Photo: pp. 95, 96.

Library of Congress Cataloging in Publication Data

Keller, Mollie.
Marie Curie.

(An Impact biography)
Bibliography: p.
Includes index.
Summary: A biography of the Polish-born chemist who was awarded the Nobel Prize in 1903 for the discovery of radium.
1. Curie, Marie, 1867–1934—
Juvenile literature.
2. Chemists—France—Biography—
Juvenile literature.
[1. Curie, Marie, 1867–1934. 2. Chemists]
QD22.C8K44   540′.92′4 [B] [92]   82-6904
ISBN 0-531-04476-9   AACR2

CONTENTS

1
THE RAW MATERIAL 1

2
PARIS 17

3
THE SEARCH 31

4
FAME 49

5
ALONE 65

6
MOVING OUT 83

7
PEACE 101

FOR FURTHER READING 117
INDEX 118

When Marie Curie, who, by discovering a
new element, opened a new age of science
and technology and forever changed
man's understanding of matter, was first
approached about writing her autobiography,
she was genuinely surprised.

"It will not be much of a book," she replied.
"It is such an uneventful, simple little story.
I was born in Warsaw of a family of teachers.
I married Pierre Curie and had two children.
I have done my work in France."

THE RAW
MATERIAL

1

Madame Sklodowska closed the door to her office behind her. Stopping only long enough to tell her teachers to carry on as usual, and to ask one of the younger ones to bring her some sheets and plenty of hot water, she went downstairs to her apartment. A messenger was sent to the boys' school a few streets away, first to alert her husband that he might have to leave class early, and then to fetch the doctor. While little girls recited their lessons in the classroom overhead on that chilly day in November 1867 in Warsaw, Mme Sklodowska gave birth to her fifth child, Marie.

All five children were bright and ambitious. Both Bronya and Joseph yearned for medical careers; Zosia seemed destined to be a writer; Hela had inherited her mother's musical talent. And Marie, who read fluently by the age of four, was endlessly fascinated by her father's physics apparatus, the assortment of pipes, test tubes, crystals, and scales locked behind the doors of the glass-fronted cabinet in the parlor.

Mr. Sklodowski*, a professor of physics and mathematics, was Marie's role model for a scientific career. His was a character well-suited for a life of experiment and evaluation. A self-con-

---

*In Polish, Sklodowski is the masculine form of the name; Sklodowska, the feminine.

trolled man, he never allowed himself (or his family) to raise their voices either in anger or in joy. Sklodowski was naturally introspective, rational, and precise. Even when he took his family on excursions, he planned their itinerary down to the minute, and prepared lectures on the various sights and shrines he wanted them to remember. He encouraged them to observe everything.

He also showed them that education is a lifelong process. Part of his modest salary went for subscriptions to scholarly journals so that he could keep up with the newest developments in the scientific world. This was a man who read Greek and Latin, and spoke English, French, German, and Russian, besides his native Polish. He spent every Saturday night reading aloud to his children, often translating into Polish as he read the original. Marie's father also wrote poetry; his interests and talents were manifold.

Madame Sklodowska was a gifted pianist and singer. Well-educated in Warsaw, she first taught at the school she later directed. But her strong sense of duty forced her to abandon her career shortly after Marie's birth. She felt she could no longer give enough time to both school and family, as her husband's new job required them to move to other quarters. Marie's mother was strong-willed and righteous. It was she who took charge of the children's religious and moral education, taking them with her to daily Mass, setting an example of goodness and charity.

She was also an excellent manager, stretching a small income to cover the needs of a family of seven. Mme Sklodowska learned the cobbler's trade so she wouldn't have to spend so much on the children's shoes. She mended and patched, cooked and cleaned. Her children never saw her sitting idly; there was always handwork in her lap.

Marie's childhood should have been ideal. What could be better than to be born to loving parents who not only understood but also nurtured her gifts? But the dark clouds that were to overshadow Marie's life quickly rolled over her horizon. Very early she learned that life was hard and often unfair, and that to achieve her dreams she would have to be patient, strong, and determined.

The most immediate shadow was that of death. Mme Sklodowska developed tuberculosis when Marie was still a toddler. The child couldn't understand why her mother never kissed her, or why she used special dishes, and sat apart from the family. Hard to bear, too, was her mother's long stay in a French hospital. While this separation did little to help Mme Sklodowska, it did help prepare her family for the inevitable final separation that came when Marie was not yet eleven.

This was Marie's second experience with death. Her eldest sister Zosia had fallen victim of a typhus epidemic; the disease had been carried to the Sklodowski home by one of the Professor's pupils. Marie could not logically accept why God had let two such innocent, devout, and good creatures suffer and die. She began to have doubts about her religion, and by her teens had left the Church for good.

If God seemed to have abandoned the family, poverty had not. Medical expenses drained most of the family's capital, and a disastrous investment took the rest. They lived solely on the Professor's salary, a wage that kept shrinking as Sklodowski lost job after job—not for incompetence, but because of politics.

Just as the Soviet Union dominates Poland today, so the Russian Empire did a century ago. Since 1773, when it had come under Russian rule, Poland had been struggling for self-determination. The Czar quashed each new rebellion and, during Marie's childhood, began to Russianize Poland with a vengeance. Polish law courts were abolished. The country was labeled on all new maps as the Russian province of "Vistula Land." The Polish language was demoted to a dialect while Russian became the "province's" official language, to be spoken at home and in public. To supervise the conversion, Russian bureaucrats replaced Polish officials.

It was this last policy that affected Sklodowski the most. He was able to teach in Russian; he was willing to forgo the Polish history lessons. But what he could bear with only despair and bitterness was always having to yield his job to less-qualified Russians. Such a perversion of justice and education did more than reduce the Sklodowskis' standard of living. It made them angry, ardent patriots. Marie herself never stopped believing that she must do all she could to free her country from the Russian oppressors.

Thus the qualities that helped Marie in her scientific career were fixed in her childhood. From her father she inherited a logical mind and a love of precision. Her mother gave her a sense of duty, honor, and the virtue of hard work. The parents' physical restraint endowed their daughter with the strength to be alone without being lonely. Their devotion to learning, reinforced by an evening ritual of lessons and study, fired the girl with ambition and taught her that life's greatest rewards were those attained with the mind.

The family's usual lack of money taught Marie how to make more out of less. She was able, even when she became older and famous, to make do with only two black dresses that were equally at home in the laboratory and drawing room. She never ate much, and was content with few possessions. Nor was she ever afraid of hardship or labor.

Poverty also sharpened Marie's powers of concentration and self-discipline. How else could she survive in a crowded apartment that echoed with the voices and dreams of her siblings and her father's students who boarded with the family? Once as she sat reading at the dining room table, head on hands, the other children erected a shaky scaffold of chairs above and around her. She heard none of their giggling and plotting. When Marie finished her chapter and stood up, the pyramid tumbled around her. But the hoped for screaming and shrieking never happened. This youngest child looked at her elder companions, quietly said, "That's stupid," and walked out of the room.

Marie was never really a childish child. Adults always said

she was older than her years because of her mature behavior. She was detached, an observer of her own life, disinterested yet fascinated—just as a good scientist should be.

There were, of course, respites from the stresses of Marie's life. She enjoyed games with her family, trips to the outdoor markets, visits with relatives who worked on vast country estates where the girl learned to ride the farm horses and roamed the woods and fields. Friends, festivals, and sleigh rides distracted her from the trials of her city life. But Marie always understood that these activities were interludes, and that life for her would mean something else. It was in school that she first realized what her life's work—and enjoyment—might be.

While her family had shown her the path to knowledge, they did not educate her themselves. Uniformed and scrubbed, she attended various girls' schools in Warsaw, always under the watchful eyes of the Russian inspectors. Two years younger than her classmates, Marie was still first in arithmetic, history, literature, German, French, and catechism. Her time in elementary school was made especially sweet by the nationalism of her teachers. One of them used to conduct illegal Polish history lessons in Polish, first being sure to post a sentry in the hall to warn the young rebels of approaching inspectors.

Marie passed easily on to the *gymnasium*, or high school. The *gymnasia* were dedicated to Russification. In fact, the one Marie attended was staffed by Germans and Russians; the only Poles in the building sat behind the students' desks. It was hard for the uncompromising Marie to play by the Russian rules, but she had to if she wanted to get the diploma that only a gymnasium could give.

Worlds opened for Marie here, new worlds of mathematics and natural science, of poetry and philosophy. In spite of being in the enemy's camp, Marie was able to confide to her best friend that ". . . I like school. Perhaps you will make fun of me, but nevertheless I must tell you that I like it, and even that I love it. I can realize that now." She had discovered the exhilaration of new ideas and the joy of stretching her mind to the fullest.

One fine day in June 1883, Marie pinned a bunch of roses to the waist of her good black dress, and set off to the *gymnasium* for the last time. She was graduating first in her class, the winner of a gold metal and a stack of Russian prize books, fifteen years old, and in a state of nervous collapse.

Although the work was easy for her, being in school was a strain for Marie. She was shy among strangers. Reciting in class was an ordeal that made her tremble and reduced her voice to a whisper. But the greatest pressure was her own drive to succeed and excel, a need nurtured in her competitive academic family. Since Joseph and Bronya had already won gold medals, how could Marie do less?

Marie called her condition that June "the fatigue of growth and study." Today we might call it a nervous breakdown. To her father the cure seemed obvious: a year with relatives in the country, with no studying allowed.

This was to be a year of sunlight for a girl who had known so much gloom. She had no obligations, no timetables, and no plans. She filled her days with excursions to find sweet wild strawberries and stolen naps in the meadows; one night at a village feast she danced right through the soles of her red shoes. Once she soothed her conscience about her idleness, she found life easy, pleasant, and even frivolous. Marie applied the same intensity to enjoying herself as she had to studying. The goal she set herself was to recover, and in her year away she regained her health and humor, and stored up enough happy memories to nourish her throughout a lifetime of overwhelming labor.

At sixteen, she returned to Warsaw and frustration. All roads to further education were blocked. The Latin and Greek essential for admission to Russian universities were taught only at boys' *gymnasia*, so that girls were automatically excluded from studying at the university. An ambitious girl had to go abroad and take a degree at a foreign university. Marie's elder sister Bronya wanted to study medicine at the Sorbonne in Paris. Marie, who saw herself following the family tradition of teaching, also wanted to complete her education at this famous French university. The only problem was finding the money to pay for it.

The Sklodowska girls decided to put their talents to work for them, and promptly set themselves up as private tutors. They figured they'd have lots of business from students who were not as well equipped as they to master the intricacies of the Russian language or educational system. Unfortunately, they were not the only young women in Warsaw to think this way. Despite her elegant handwritten cards ("Lessons in arithmetic, geometry, French, by a young lady with diploma. Moderate fees."), Marie spent a lot of time sitting at home, waiting for the customers who rarely came.

Marie had made up her mind to make enough money to send first Bronya, then herself to Paris. Her plan worked well in theory, but Marie had overlooked the fact that not everyone was as eager for knowledge as she. The idealistic girl was not prepared for stupid and lazy pupils, for long tramps in freezing rain to meet with a student who kept her waiting for an hour in a drafty hall, for being treated as a servant, and worst of all, for clients who "forgot" to pay her at the end of the month.

At half a rouble a lesson it was hardly surprising that Marie couldn't save much money. Family finances were no better than they had been. Dresses were mended, patched, and finally made over. Again the family moved to smaller quarters, and trimmed the budget yet another time. But Paris was still as far away as ever.

So as not to waste those hours not given to tutoring or chores, Marie began attending a clandestine arrangement of lectures called the "floating university." It "floated" because its small classes in anatomy or sociology had to meet in different attics, basements, or living rooms each week in order to elude the spies of the state police. As a Polish school operating outside the Rus-

sian system, this university was illegal and its students and teachers liable to arrest. The staff included professional teachers who were willing to risk a long winter in Siberia for the joy of sharing their knowledge with these ardent adolescents, as well as a few radicals and enthusiasts whose ideas were not always as well developed as their zeal.

The floating university had another aim besides educating high school graduates. It sought to turn its students into teachers. Marie, struggling to overcome her shyness, chose to read aloud to the girls who worked at a nearby dressmaker's shop, and soon collected a small Polish library for their use. For doing this, she was just as guilty of treason as her teachers.

What made a girl of seventeen accept such a risk? The idealism of youth, the intoxication of knowledge, the fervor of patriotism were all factors. But most of all it was because this floating university gave her a philosophy upon which she could build her life. In those secret sessions, Marie found her religion and purpose.

The philosophy was positivism. As originated by Auguste Comte fifty years earlier, the system rejected theoretical speculation about man and his problems in favor of positive, observable, scientific facts and their relation to each other and natural law. The positivists believed in reason and logic. Charles Darwin and Louis Pasteur were their heroes, for hadn't they applied scientific methods to human questions? Scientific discipline would surely provide the solutions to society's ills. The goals of Marie's positivist friends sound surprisingly like the ideals of today's liberal

Marie Sklodowska (left) is shown here with her sister Bronya, about the time the two young women were trying to earn money tutoring in Warsaw.

youth: women's rights; an end to discrimination; economic opportunity for all. They believed that they would change the world.

Positivism filled the hole left in Marie's life by her rejection of the Church, and gave her a god she could understand and serve gladly: science. She took her credo from a Polish poet:

> Look for the clear light of Truth;
> Look for unknown new roads . . .
> Every age has its own dreams,
> Leave, then, the dreams of yesterday;
> You—take the torch of knowledge,
> Perform a new work among the labors of the centuries
> And build the palace of the future. . . .

But ideals do not pay tuition. For all her zeal, Marie's savings had not grown. Bronya had managed to save enough money to get herself to Paris, and if Marie were to follow, she would have to find real work. Her solution was to become a governess. With room and board supplied by her employers, Marie hoped to save all her salary for her education fund.

Her first job was with a lawyer's family. But Marie did not adapt well to what she saw as their empty lives, malicious gossip, and immoral behavior. The highly principled young positivist soon told her employers that she could not work for people she did not respect. She was promptly fired.

The second post took her seven hours by train and sleigh into the Polish countryside. While her new employers were pleasant, attractive, and kind, their estate in the country turned out to be in the heart of the sugar beet district. Instead of snowy fields and sparkling evergreens, all Marie could see from the small window of her attic room were the black chimneys of the dark brick factories where the beets were processed into sugar, and the ramshackle cottages of the peasants. Any open land was either planted with this year's crop or waiting, raw and muddy, for next year's crop. The beets even stained the river pink.

To Marie's disappointment, her pupil was lazy and undisciplined. Marie often had to pull her out of bed. Nor was it easy for Marie to find friends. The young people she met spoke only of neighbors and parties—not a word of philosophy or science. Fighting against her strait-laced disapproval of such behavior, Marie forced herself to stay and, in time, found compensations.

On one of her walks with her pupil she followed the muddy lanes to a village, and saw dirty little children staring from the dark doorways of their tiny cottages. These were peasant children, Polish children for Marie to teach. Here was her chance to practice the ideals she had brought from Warsaw. With her employers' permission (given in full recognition of the dangers of such subversive activity), Marie set up a school.

Every day after her regular seven or eight hours of duty, Marie welcomed ten ragged children who timidly climbed the outside stairway to her room. She gave them pens and stiff new notebooks. With clumsy fingers grasping the slender instruments, slowly and laboriously the children learned to scratch out the sounds they spoke and heard. They were the first in their village to read.

Within a year the class had grown to eighteen pupils and Marie was spending an extra five hours a day in her secret school. She also visited her students' homes, dark hovels brimming with starving children, so different from the warmth and light of the home of the factory owner she worked for. Marie had read *Das Kapital* and recognized this gap between worker and capitalist as just what Marx had described, but she rejected communism. She didn't care about the workers of the world, only about Poles and Poland. Besides, she had her priorities elsewhere. She didn't want to pursue politics, only science.

Mindful of her future at the Sorbonne and well-trained in the habit of self-education, Marie called up reserves of intellectual and physical energy and began to use the leftover hours of her day for study. She wanted to explore the realms of physics and mathematics she had glimpsed at the floating university. Her concentration and persistence soon had her getting up earlier and going to bed later in order to have more time to read. She stopped accompanying her employers to parties or playing cards in the evenings because she could use the time for study instead. Without realizing it, she had begun her life's work.

After three years at this post, and after an ill-fated romance with her employers' son, Marie returned to Warsaw, tutoring, and her university. But now she was no longer learning chemistry only from books; now she could try the experiments she read about. A cousin had found her a laboratory where she could go at night and on Sundays to teach herself the basic skills of physical science: how to handle thermometers; use an electroscope to measure tiny electrical charges; distill a clear liquid from a muddy mixture. Difficult as these sessions were, they pleased her more than anything she had ever known. She later wrote of her first adventures in the laboratory: "Though I was taught that the way of progress is neither swift nor easy, this first trial confirmed me in the taste for experimental research."

For all the thrill of her new discoveries, she still longed for Paris. Hard work and waiting had worn her down, however, and she was too tired to care if she ever went. In fact, she turned down her sister's first invitation to live with her in Paris, blaming her action on their father's declining health.

But when Bronya wrote again the next year, Marie was ready. She realized that she was almost twenty-four and it was time for her to start living for herself.

Professor Sklodowski poses with his daughters Marie (far left), Bronya, and Hela for a family portrait made in 1890, the year before Marie went to Paris.

A few days after getting Bronya's letter, Marie counted her money. She had just enough for a year in Paris. Quickly she packed her mattress, sheets, blankets, and table linen, and sent them on ahead. Hurrying now, so she wouldn't miss the opening of the term, she bought a strong wooden trunk, marked it M.S., and put in her serviceable dresses, her shoes, and her two hats. On her last day at home she readied her provisions for the long train ride across Europe: meals for the three-day trip, a wooden camp stool to sit on so she wouldn't have to pay extra for a seat, her books, an extra blanket, and a bag of caramels.

Who was this young woman who struggled with bags and bundles on the platform of the Warsaw station? An assortment of dreams, a mixture of determination and shyness, a blend of intelligence and ignorance. Short and plump, with her waist pulled in by a tight corset and her curly hair piled untidily on top of her head, she was an ordinary looking woman with an extraordinary goal—a proper scientific university education—and the strength to achieve it.

Chance had given her a background that forged her independence and ambition. A disciplined upbringing, poverty, personal loss, and sporadic and diverse education had shaped and fixed her character long before she boarded her Paris-bound train. Whatever else fate might present her with, Marie Sklodowska was her own person.

PARIS

2

Marie must have felt as if she had landed on another planet when she got off the train in Paris. Outside the station, streets bustled with shoppers and strollers, and store windows glittered with trinkets and toys. Clouds of children brushed past her on their way to school, jabbering and teasing in their own language. Bookstalls overflowed with volumes brimming with ideas from all over the world. No one looked over his shoulder for a secret policeman. This city and its citizens were confident, vital, and free.

Balancing her bags and bundles, Marie made her way to the apartment where her sister Bronya and her husband, Casimir Dluski, lived and practiced medicine. She was going to stay with them, not far from the station serving the trains that could carry her back to Poland in case Paris proved too much for her. The neighborhood was inhabited primarily by French butchers and Polish émigrés and students. Entering Bronya's apartment was just like coming home. There were Polish books on the shelves, Polish pictures on the walls, Polish talk around the table and everywhere the smells of Polish cooking. Bronya's home was a familiar base from which Marie could venture out to explore the city in the morning and to which she could return gratefully at night.

She arrived in November 1891, just in time for the start of the fall term. On the first day of class, following her sister's thrifty advice, Marie climbed to the open top of the horse-bus (where the satisfaction of the cheaper fare more than made up for the discomfort of the occasional rainstorm) and began the long trip to the Sorbonne. The panorama of Paris rolled by at the horse's steady gait. Marie saw elegant new buildings gracing streets bright with modern electric lights; watched women in stylish gowns and plumed hats on their way to a couturier or café; marveled at a few strange and noisy vehicles in the roads that were propelled neither by man nor beast, but by internal combustion engines. Across the rooftops she glimpsed the ancient spires of Notre Dame and the tricolored French flag waving gaily from the newest wonder of engineering ingenuity, the Eiffel Tower. Hugging her old leather briefcase, she strained to see the Sorbonne as the bus crept through the Latin Quarter along the Boulevard Saint Michel. At last she was there. The dream she had cherished for so long was about to come true.

Students had been coming to the Sorbonne from all over Europe since the Middle Ages. By 1891, its buildings were due for a facelift, and when Marie got there, spidery scaffolding covered the walls of the old structures. Classes migrated from room to room as workmen moved in to modernize the lecture halls. But the dust, noise, and confusion could not dampen Marie's delight. Each day she was the first to arrive at the lectures so she could get a front row seat. Neatly she set out her pens and notebooks, then sat quietly waiting for the professor. Her teachers included some of the most famous scientists and mathematicians of the day, and they led her into realms far more fascinating than any she had ever found in a fairy tale. Her favorite mathematics professor was Paul Appell, who once thrilled Marie by beginning a class with the words: ''I take the sun and throw it. . . .''

Exciting as her classes were, they were not without problems for the Polish girl. She had come to Paris for a Master's Degree in physics with a command of the French language that had never been actually tried on a Frenchman. To her dismay, the professors spoke in rapid technical French that left Marie struggling at the beginning of a sentence while the rest of the class was at the end of a paragraph. Even more serious was her lack of a solid foundation in physics and mathematics. The almost haphazard scientific education she had acquired through the floating university, her father's tutoring, and her own explorations in that Warsaw laboratory could not compare with the training her classmates had received in French high schools and colleges.

But Marie was not discouraged. She simply made up her mind to fill in the holes herself, and with stubborn determination dedicated herself entirely to study. When she wasn't doing her class assignments, she was busy making up for lost years, reading scientific texts never available to her before. Just as she had done during her governess days, she began to regard every minute away from her books as wasted time. This new attitude forced her to reconsider her situation and habits.

Living with Bronya was comfortable and comforting, but very distracting. Almost every night guests filled the apartment with talk and smoke, or else her brother-in-law insisted Marie accompany them to some party or concert. Her new regimen left no time for such diversions, no matter how pleasant, relaxing, or important to her mental health they might be. Nor did it allow for the long trip from the Dluskis' home to the Sorbonne. The two hours she spent on the bus each day could be better spent in the library or laboratory.

Marie decided to live closer to school, in the Latin Quarter itself, where she would be only a short walk from the lecture halls. Since the university did not provide dormitories or dining halls, its neighborhood catered to the thousands of students who thronged the area. There were cheap lodgings and even cheaper cafés where the young people could meet, eat, and argue politics or philosophy at all hours. If she needed or wanted to, Marie would be close to classmates and colleagues who could offer an extra dimension to her education.

Early in 1892, the Dluskis helped her move into her first apartment—an attic room, lit only by a skylight, with no heat and no water. It was as much as Marie could afford on her hundred franc a month allowance if she intended to eat, too. She furnished her new home with an iron bed, a stove, a table, one chair, two lamps, two plates, a knife, fork, and spoon, one cup, one stew-pan, and one kettle. Her sister Bronya's housewarming present was three glasses, so that she and her husband could have tea when they came to call. Marie also had a bucket to carry water from the tap on the landing, and a scuttle to fetch coal from the basement. The few visitors who found their way up the six flights of stairs to Marie's room were offered seats on her wooden trunk, tea out of one of the three glasses, and rarely stayed long.

That was fine with Marie. Obsessed by her studies, she had no need for company. So jealous was she of her peace and privacy, it hadn't even occurred to her that she could live more comfortably and more cheaply with a roommate to share expenses.

Her devotion to her work helped her ignore the physical dis-comforts of her life, too. She refused to wilt in the stifling heat of her room in the summer, and in the winter would read in dim light and finger-numbing cold rather than spend her small and costly rations of oil and coal. On nights cold enough to freeze the water in her wash basin, Marie would go to bed with all her clothes on, and balance her chair on top of the bedclothes to give herself the illusion of warmth, rather than light the stove.

Marie had little housework to do, and she never bothered to cook. How could she justify taking time from a physics problem to scramble an egg? Her diet consisted of finger food—bread, radishes, fruit, and a rare piece of chocolate. On more than one occasion she fainted from hunger in the classroom, and once became so weak and ill that she had to be carried back to the Dluskis' for a week of forced rest and feeding. Back on her own, of course, she resumed her unhealthy habits.

Marie also existed with very little sleep. She rose at dawn in order to get in a couple of hours' study before attending the morning lecture. Her afternoons were spent in the laboratory where, with a rumpled linen smock pulled over her well-mended dress, she might construct some delicate apparatus or watch the slow precipitation of a mysterious substance. She worked quietly and amiably with her fellow students, all of whom were equally absorbed in their test tubes and thermometers.

But when their experiments were finished and the scientists took off their lab coats and became young students again, Marie kept to herself. Too shy to initiate a friendship and too reserved to allow even a good friend to call her by her first name, Marie never sought the companionship of her colleagues. She went back to her room to study alone until the light began to fail. Then, rather than waste her own fuel, she went to the warm and well-lit St. Genevieve library where she read until its ten P.M. closing. After that she only needed enough oil to keep her lamp lit until two A.M., when she would finally allow herself to go to bed. If she ever found herself too tired to study, Marie relaxed by washing her clothes or mending her stockings.

Marie stuck to her schedule with an iron will. She pushed herself to her limits to get her education, ignoring the discomforts, privations, and loneliness of her life. Nothing mattered to her but her passion for knowledge; the only world she fully lived in was the scientific one. She explained her single-minded dedication in a letter to her brother Joseph: "We must believe that we are gifted for something, and that this thing, at whatever cost, must be attained."

Despite the hardships, these were the most special days of Marie's life. Proud of her independence and intellectual efforts, she cherished their memory, and captured their spirit in a poem she wrote in Polish in one of her physics notebooks:

Harsh and hard she lived to learn.
Round her swirled the young who seek
Pleasures easy, pleasures stern.
She alone, long week by week,
Happy, gay, made great her heart.

As a student at the Sorbonne, Marie
spent many hours working in the laboratory.

When fleeting time took her away
From lands of knowledge and of art
To earn her bread on life's grey way,
Oft times her spirit sighed to know.
Again the attic corner strait,
Still scene of silent labor slow,
So filled with memory of fate.

Marie progressed through a curriculum of calculus to physics to mechanics and electrostatics, and with each course grew in comprehension and skill. Driven to do her best, and impatient with anything less than perfection from herself, Marie did not feel competent enough to take the degree examination until the spring of 1893. Even then she made herself sick with anxiety, convincing herself that she would fail. But when the results were announced, Marie ranked first in her class. Hard work and determination had earned her fluency in both French and physics. Her triumph meant that she could have the scientific career she wanted, instead of having to go back to being a governess in the Polish countryside.

Her success also strengthened her secret resolve to obtain a second Master's Degree in mathematics. Working in physics and chemistry labs had shown her how essential a solid mathematical background was to a fruitful life in research. She had kept this ambition secret because, unaware of the extent of her remarkable talents, she was afraid she wasn't capable enough to get it.

Before continuing her studies, however, Marie spent all that was left of her money on presents for her family and went back to Warsaw for a long relaxing summer vacation. Well-rested and well-fed, she returned to Paris in the fall, her suitcase containing two new dresses to replace the old ones her sister Hela had stuffed into the ragbag as soon as she'd unpacked them. Marie's purse contained more money, too—the Alexandrovitch Scholarship awarded six hundred roubles to deserving Polish students who wanted to study abroad. So grateful was Marie for this grant that she paid it back out of the salary from her first research job, so that some other scholar might have the same opportunities she did.

The scholarship financed another garret room and another year of rigorous study. In the spring, Marie ranked second among the candidates for the mathematics degree. Thus, within three years of her hopeful arrival in Paris, through her diligence, dedication, and natural brilliance, she had achieved her dream of a strong scientific education. As a student at the Sorbonne, she had lived an enchanted life, removed from all material and emotional concerns. But now what was she going to do with her hard-won education?

Certainly she intended to return to Warsaw for the summer of '94 to rest, visit her family, and enjoy her academic laurels. Perhaps she would stay and teach in Poland; no Pole, she felt, had a right to abandon her country and, besides, she missed her father.

There were, however, strong forces pulling her back to Paris. One was her growing reputation as a researcher and analytical scientist. Even before she completed her second degree, her professors had given her research jobs to provide her with both experience and income. One of these assignments also gave her something far more important, something that was to be her greatest reason for returning to France.

Early in 1894, the Society for the Encouragement of National Industry commissioned Marie to develop a thesis about the magnetic properties of different kinds of steel. It was an important opportunity, but the laboratory facilities Marie had at the Sorbonne were sadly inadequate for the job. She needed a lot more space and special equipment. One of her teachers knew the head of the laboratory of the School of Physics and Chemistry of the City of Paris and thought he might be able to help. Her teacher arranged for Marie to meet the man one afternoon at tea. His name was Pierre Curie.

Pierre Curie was then thirty-five years old. He had already made a name for himself as a brilliant physicist. His work on the principles of symmetry in crystals was pioneering in modern science. Yet while scientists from all over the world came to Paris to consult with him, he received very little recognition from his own countrymen. His job at the laboratory paid well, but it was still a wage well below that of the professors of his school. Pierre was content with his position, however, because it let him do the one thing he lived for—scientific research.

Pierre had had an unusual upbringing. His father, a doctor who pursued both a medical practice and research, understood that his son's genius and temperament would not flourish in a conventional school and chose to tutor the boy himself, at home. Pierre was left free to indulge his love of mathematics at his own pace. Looking for beauty and order in a seemingly chaotic world, he tried to apply mathematical laws to natural phenomena. His observations of symmetry in flowers, animals, and sea shells led him into his search for symmetry in crystals as well. At sixteen he earned his Bachelor of Science Degree, and he had his Master's in physics at eighteen. He achieved so much so quickly because he was given the time and freedom to let his mind wander, contemplate, and formulate.

He was also helped by the intellectual and emotional companionship of his brother Jacques. Together they found that when certain crystals were compressed they developed an electric charge and, conversely, that an electric current could make these same crystals expand and contract. They called this conversion of mechanical to electrical energy *piezoelectricity* (*piezen* means to press in Greek). Pierre and Jacques used these piezoelectric crystals to build a very sensitive electrometer that could measure very tiny amounts of electricity. Other piezoelectric crystals are now used in microphones, radios, and electronic circuits.

By himself, Pierre had formulated Curie's Law, which states that the magnetic properties of substances change at certain temperatures (the Curie point). The development of modern telephone, telegraph, radio, and television equipment is based on a knowledge of these temperatures. Pierre had also built a delicate balance scale that could weigh tiny bits of material quickly and accurately.

While other scientists applied Pierre's work to specific problems, Pierre himself was not interested. Unconcerned for his material comforts, he sold the patent for the balance scale to a chemical company and showed no desire to benefit from any other of his theories or inventions. Pierre turned his back on wealth and fame, refusing any honors, prizes, or lucrative positions that came his way, explaining that "nothing is more unhealthy for the spirit than preoccupations of that kind." From his insatiable need to understand the natural world, he had eliminated anything in his life that might interfere with his search for a scientific truth which, he believed, "once found, can't disappear and can never be wrong."

Perhaps it was this shared ambition that attracted Marie to the physicist. Or perhaps it was his serious charm, enhanced by the elegance of his lanky body and long sensitive hands. A pointed beard lengthened his thin face; his hair was cropped in a spiky crew cut; his eyes were calm and contemplative. Naturally reserved, a man who never raised his voice, Pierre must have reminded Marie of her own father.

Within minutes of their introduction Pierre and Marie were discoursing easily about their work and goals. Pierre was surprised at this thin young girl in her shabby dress, with her flyaway hair, serious expression, and fingers badly stained by chemicals. He had long ago discarded love and marriage for himself, confiding to his diary that "women of genius are rare" and that "when we give all our thoughts to some great work which separates us from the ordinary life around us, we have literally to fight against woman." He had never before met any female so free of coquetry, who also shared his enthusiasm for the intellectual life, and who understood what he meant when he said that "the only dream man should live for was the scientific dream."

Pierre asked to see her again, and many times during the winter and spring of 1894 he climbed to Marie's garret to discuss first their work and, later on, their futures. The first gift he sent her was not flowers or candy, but a copy of an article he had written about magnetic fields. Not what every girl might want, perhaps, but just the right present for Marie. Their courtship had begun.

Both Pierre and Marie had decided to forgo family life for their vocations. Now they began to see that they might have both, for each inspired and encouraged the other. Marie urged Pierre to finish his doctorate, and listened as he worked out his hypotheses and theories; he in turn helped her with her steel experiments.

By August 1894, Pierre had begun proposing marriage in eloquent letters that followed the indecisive Marie from Paris to her father's house in Warsaw, and back to Paris where she returned to work on a teaching certificate. Still scarred by her unhappy romance during her governess days and afraid of being hurt again, Marie wasn't sure she wanted to share her career or life with anyone. Nor did she feel comfortable about leaving Poland forever.

Pierre had no doubts, however. He knew that theirs would be a wonderful marriage and scientific partnership, and he redoubled his efforts in 1895. He took her home to meet his parents; he visited the Dluskis to enlist their help in persuading Marie to accept him. He suggested renting a large apartment that could be divided in half so that they could live and work together even if they didn't get married. Finally he offered to give up his work and move to Poland in order to be with her. "It would be a fine thing. . ." he wrote, "in which I hardly dare believe, to pass our lives near each other, hypnotised by our dreams: *your* patriotic dream, *our* humanitarian dream, and *our* scientific dream."

Marie finally agreed to marry Pierre and live in France. As she explained in a letter written to a girlhood friend in Poland just a few days before her marriage: "It is a sorrow to me to have to stay forever in Paris, but what am I to do? Fate has made us deeply attached to each other and we cannot endure the idea of separating."

They were married on July 26, 1895, in the city hall at Sceaux, the small town where Pierre's parents lived. There were no guests at the civil ceremony besides the Curies, the Dluskis, Marie's father, and her sister Hela. The couple was too poor to provide a wedding breakfast—they couldn't even afford wedding rings—and, in fact, had arrived at the city hall after a long early morning ride on bus and train. Marie wore a new navy blue suit with a blue-striped blouse, a gift from Bronya's mother-in-law. Characteristically, she had declined the offer of a traditional wedding dress, writing that "If you are going to be kind enough to give me one, please let it be practical and dark, so that I can put it on afterwards to go to the laboratory."

The ceremony over, the couple got on the shiny new bicycles they had purchased the day before with wedding present money, and pedaled off on a honeymoon in the French countryside. The two dedicated scientists had acknowledged their need for something in their lives besides science, and had committed themselves to a sharing of all facets of their emotional and intellectual lives. Pierre and Marie were bound by more than temperament, ideals, and interests. They were also bound by love.

THE SEARCH

3

Pierre and Marie wandered through tiny villages the whole of August, stopping at rustic inns and generous farms for food and rest. Sometimes they would leave their bicycles at the side of the road and tramp through woods and fields. Pierre, a gifted naturalist whose eyes were always open for a flower or insect he had never seen before, would talk about a physics problem, testing a new idea on the ready and perceptive ears of his bride, and then stop suddenly to fashion a crown of iris for her hair, or to make her a present of a wet wiggly frog.

But two such serious and compulsive workers could not stay idle for long. Eager to structure their new life together, they returned to their three-room apartment in early September. Marie wrote later that Pierre could never be far from his laboratory. Each time they took a vacation he would say after only a few day's rest: "It seems to me a very long time since we have accomplished anything," and they would turn their bicycles back toward Paris.

Pierre and Marie had agreed to keep their home as simple as possible so that they would have more time for their work. Marie declined her in-laws' offer of furniture. A rug, a sofa, or even an extra chair beyond what they needed would mean dusting, cleaning and, worst of all, entertaining even one uninvited and unwelcome visitor. The Curies had two chairs, a table to work and eat at, a lamp, a bookshelf, and a bed. The apartment's only decoration was a vase kept filled with fresh flowers.

The couple lived and worked and studied together. Marie was allowed to use the lab at Pierre's school for the research she was doing for her teaching certificate. But besides being a chemist and a physicist, Marie found she had to be a domestic scientist as well, for when she took Pierre's name, she also took on all the responsibilities of running his home. She attacked the mysteries of housekeeping as thoroughly as she had done everything else. Realizing that a balanced budget made a happy home, she purchased a black notebook with the word "Accounts" stamped on the cover in gold letters. In this book, and all those that followed it, she recorded *all* the quantifiable details of her life. Every centime spent on jam or cheese, every franc for rent or bicycle tires was listed without comment by the cool hand of a trained scientist.

She put her training to use in the kitchen as well. Marie understood that her diet of air and water would not suit her new life or her husband's health. The problem was that she had never learned to cook. Other Polish students used to joke that "Mlle Sklodowska doesn't even know what goes into soup!" Emergency lessons from Bronya did little to alleviate Marie's fears of displeasing Pierre (who fortunately rarely noticed what he ate) and seeming incompetent to her French mother-in-law. Treating this as she would any other research problem, Marie began to study her cookbooks, diligently trying recipes and annotating the pages to indicate their success or failure. Eventually she invented dishes that she could assemble early in the morning and leave to cook all day over a gas flame whose height she carefully calculated and adjusted.

Pierre and Marie created a quiet life to fit their interests and habits. They rose early, he to read, she to market for and prepare the evening meal. Then, arm in arm, they walked to the laboratory to spend the day working just a few feet away from each other. On the way home they shopped for the vegetables for their dinner, perhaps bought the evening paper, and then, returning to their private world, they cleared the physics papers off the table, ate, and studied in companionable silence until very late at night. They needed no other company, no worldly relations, no other diversions. They had each other and their science. Neither could imagine a more perfect mate.

After Marie passed her final exams for the teaching certificate in first place in August 1896, the Curies immediately set off on a much-needed vacation. They returned, refreshed and relaxed, to another year of work, but one that was to be complicated by the fatal illness of Pierre's mother and by the uncomfortable fact of Marie's pregnancy. Although she and Pierre wanted a baby very much, Marie was impatient with the nausea and dizziness that kept her from standing at the lab bench for eight hours a day and resentful of having to curtail her bicycle rides with Pierre. She tried to ignore her discomfort as she had done all her other ailments, even to the point of taking a long cycling tour the month before the baby was due. Not surprisingly, they had to cut the trip short and hurry back to Paris where, on September 12, 1897, Irène Curie was delivered by her grandfather. The event was duly recorded in Marie's account book under the heading "Unusual Expense: Champagne 3 fr; Telegrams 1 fr 50."

Now Marie had four things to drain her time: her work, her home, her husband, and her baby. No one ever asked her to give up her career to manage these other responsibilities, nor did Marie think to do it. The Curies simply hired a nurse to watch Irène while Marie went back to the laboratory. But the demands of motherhood still intruded on her work. How could she study at home if the baby was crying, and how could she conduct her experiments if part of her mind was wondering whether the nurse had somehow lost the baby?

Marie relaxed somewhat when her father-in-law moved in with them after his wife's death and became the nurse that she could trust completely. Marie was then able to concentrate all her powers on her scientific career. Her report on steel that had brought Pierre into her life was almost ready for publication; she already had two degrees and a certificate. But now she saw the next stage not as simply settling down to teach physics to young women, but as studying for a doctorate in science.

What seems now to be a logical development in her career was, at the time, a radical suggestion. No woman in Europe had yet completed this degree, although others had tried and failed. The conflicting social demands of family and the scientific demands of research required a strength and will few Victorian women possessed. Marie understood that to get her degree she would have to compete on a man's terms—no concessions for delicate health or maternal duties—with the extra burden of overcoming centuries of male prejudice. With supreme self-confidence and unshakable ambition, Marie welcomed the challenge.

The only difficulty she acknowledged was choosing a topic for her thesis. To be awarded the title of "Doctor" she would have to discover something unknown before, or solve a problem no one had yet managed to crack. The subject Marie chose changed her life, her career, and the world.

From her vantage point in 1897, Marie could survey the astonishing range of developments in scientific thought and practice that characterized the nineteenth century. The remarkable inventions of Bell and Edison, and the pioneering theories of Darwin and Pasteur ushered in a new age, one of new knowledge and creative criticism tempered by doubts and shaken beliefs. If these new ideas were right, then many conventional explanations for natural phenomena were wrong. Might that not mean that other scientific truths were also wrong? Might there not be other new laws and facts to be discovered?

The possibility excited the biologists, chemists, and physicists of the nineteenth century the way the idea of the Northwest Passage inspired the explorers of the sixteenth. With unparalleled energy, enthusiasm, and creativity they dedicated themselves to the holy cause of Science, aiming to serve humanity by increasing its knowledge. Each discovery, no matter what its size or scope, could shed light on some other problem, and with each new illumination would come greater enlightenment. Scientists worked together, complementing this one's research or inspiring that one's imagination, in a brotherhood only occasionally marred by rivalry and competition.

Perhaps no branch of science benefited more from this activity than physics, for these fertile imaginations made possible the atomic age. One man saw something and reported it to the world. Another man tried to explain the report, and his experiments intrigued a determined young woman so much that she decided to follow them up. In this way atomic physics was born.

Until 1895 very few physicists or chemists were interested in studying atoms. They knew that an atom was the smallest particle of an element, and that these atoms combined and recombined to form the myriad compounds our world is made of. In fact, chemists were so familiar with the behavior of atoms that one of them, Dmitri Mendeleyev, was able to arrange them in a periodic table that showed at a glance their relative size and characteristics. But no one, especially physicists, knew why or how atoms behaved as they did. And since there didn't seem to be any way of finding out (how can you analyze what you can't see or feel?), atomics was pretty much left out of the mainstream of scientific investigation.

A happy accident changed all that. In 1895 a professor in Germany named Wilhelm Röntgen was experimenting with electrical rays and discovered that they could fog a photographic plate, even if that plate were tightly wrapped in black paper to protect it against all light. In other words, the high-voltage was producing emissions that could penetrate paper; soon he found that they could pass through wood and flesh, too. These mysterious rays, which Röntgen dubbed X rays, also electrically charged the air around them. He quickly published his findings along with photographs of metal weights sealed inside a wooden box. Within days, surgeons in Europe and America were using X rays to look into the human body and find breaks or bullets. While the public at large joked that X rays would mean the end of privacy and modesty, fearing that they would be used to see through locked doors or layers of petticoats, the scientific community embraced X rays whole-heartedly and joined in the search for their source.

It was a Frenchman named Henri Becquerel who, reading about these rays, decided to find out if they were related to fluorescence, a property which makes some crystals glow after being exposed to light. Working methodically in his laboratory at the Paris Museum of Natural History, Becquerel tried to duplicate Röntgen's results by exposing various naturally fluorescent substances to sunlight and then placing them near a photographic plate wrapped in black paper. Nothing he tested fogged the plates until he used a uranium compound. Becquerel concluded that he had found some fluorescent X rays.

Before he rushed into print with his discovery, he repeated the experiments to make sure of his results. But the sun refused to shine that day, or for several days after, and in disgust Becquerel tossed the plates, paper, and uranium crystals into a drawer. When the weather finally broke, he decided to develop the plates anyway, figuring that a blank plate would prove that light was necessary for this phenomenon. But to his surprise the plates were fogged. He tried it again in a darkroom and the same thing happened—still the crystals sent out their rays. Clearly he'd been wrong. The emanations had nothing to do with light but were spontaneous emissions from the crystals themselves.

Further investigations proved that these rays were a property of all uranium compounds. Becquerel also observed that, like the X rays, the radiations of uranium gave the surrounding air a weak but measurable electrical conductivity. The purer the sample of uranium, the stronger the rays. But where were they coming from?

Becquerel's question was the spark that fired Marie Curie's imagination. His observations provided her with a defined research problem—to find the source of these rays—and an open field to work in. Because they could not photograph bones, Becquerel's rays never got the publicity of Röntgen's, and no one had followed up his research in the year-and-a-half since he had first published his results. Here was the opportunity for Marie to do her original work with little chance of being beaten out by an ardent competitor.

This was just the sort of challenge she loved. She would be an explorer, setting off into an unknown land, carefully recording and describing the strange new sights she found there. With diligence and determination she would discover just what these radiations were and explain them to the world.

But where was she to work? She had no job that would give her access to a good laboratory, and no money to rent one. Nor did Pierre have a lab of his own to share with her. He had to ask for the use of a little glassed-in storeroom on the ground floor of the School of Physics. The director, who was not at all interested in Marie's project, and fully expected her to abandon it and her thesis within a few weeks, gave his grudging consent. Marie got her lab, a tumbledown place full of spiders, broken machines, and leftover lumber. There was no electricity, no heat, and no equipment. Fortunately, Marie had learned from her husband's example that "one could work happily even in very insufficient quarters."

Into this abandoned space Marie moved a table, an ionization chamber, an electrometer, and a piezoelectric quartz. She intended to begin her study with an analysis of the rays' "power of ionization," that is, their capacity to make the air a conductor of electricity. For this she used an electroscope like the one she had learned on long ago in Warsaw. As she explained: "I employed . . . a plate condenser, one of the plates being covered with a uniform layer of uranium or of another finely pulverized substance. The current that traversed the condenser was measured in absolute value by means of an electrometer and a piezoelectric quartz." Her experiments must have been doubly satisfying because she was using equipment that had been invented and built by her husband and brother-in-law.

Her first results came quickly. Within two months she found that the intensity of this ionizing radiation was proportional to the amount of uranium in her sample. This was true no matter how she tried to alter the uranium with heat, light, or chemical reaction. Nothing she did affected the rays.

Marie considered and reconsidered this, and eventually hypothesized that this mysterious radiation must be an *atomic* property. The rays were the result of something that was happening within the atom itself. Although she could not know it then, this realization was to be the most important of all her work, for it led her and other scientists to explore and understand the internal structure of atoms.

Next she tested all the other known elements, either in their pure state or in compound, to see if they had the same capacity. She soon found that only the rare, grayish element thorium behaved the same way. Since this was obviously not the property of just one element, it needed a general name. Marie suggested *radioactivity* from the Latin word for ray (*radius*), and called uranium and thorium *radioelements*.

She went on with her search for radioactivity, testing salts, oxides, and compounds with her electrometer. Only those with thorium or uranium passed her test and, as she had expected, the strength of the rays depended on the amount of radioelement present. But when she asked Pierre to gather mineral samples from the physics school for her to test, she had quite a surprise. Three minerals with these two elements—glittering green chalcocite, yellow uranite, and crumbly dark pitchblende—were indeed radioactive, but their radioactivity was far greater than the amounts of thorium or uranium could warrant.

Could she have made a mistake? Marie was well aware of the difficult conditions she had to work in. Drafts and dust frequently made her instruments inaccurate and forced her to repeat her procedures. Cold (one day she recorded a temperature indoors of 6.25 degrees Celsius) and humidity negated her results, so naturally she first thought that there was an error in the experiment. She repeated the tests, and then tried them again. Each time the results were the same.

The only explanation was that there must be a new and much more powerfully radioactive substance in these minerals than either uranium or thorium. But what? She'd tested all the known elements. Was she going to discover a new one?

By April 1898, she was confident enough in her work to announce to the Academy of Science the probable presence of a new highly radioactive element in pitchblende ores. The first step was taken. Now she would have to prove her hypothesis. By isolating this element, refining and weighing it, she would give the world tangible proof of its existence.

At this point Pierre put aside his work on crystals (temporarily, he thought) and joined his wife in the laboratory, forming one of the most celebrated collaborations in the history of science. In the early summer of 1898 they began their search for the new element. They knew it must be present in very tiny amounts or it would have been identified in previous chemical analyses of pitchblende. Pierre and Marie figured conservatively that it would be one part in a hundred. What would they have done if they realized at the start that their quarry was not even a *millionth* part of the ore?

They worked with pitchblende because it showed the greatest radioactivity. As they knew none of the chemical properties of the element they were looking for, they had to find it by its rays. The Curies developed a method that has since been used to find other radioelements. Patiently they refined the pitchblende into its separate elements by grinding the ore, boiling it with acids and chemicals, and filtering this slushy mixture. Then they tested both the liquid and the residue, and threw away the part that showed no radioactivity. They saved the part that did give off rays and, using the same methods, broke it down into still simpler compounds, and finally into its component elements. In this way they hoped to trace the rays to their source.

But at the final separation they found emanations from two products of the pitchblende refining. That July they announced the existence of a new metal four hundred times more radioactive than uranium, that was chemically related to bismuth. Holding fast to Marie's patriotic dream, they called it polonium, "from the name of the original country of one of us." And the following December they told the world about radium which behaved like barium in chemical operations. Its radioactivity, even in compounds, was nine hundred times greater than uranium's. The experiments also showed them that they would need tons of pitchblende to get even the tiniest samples of these new elements.

Desperately wanting to get on with the search, the Curies felt themselves handicapped by no proper place to work, no money, and no personnel. No individual or institution offered them any help. Pierre and Marie used their small savings to buy supplies and equipment, and split the workload between them.

As for space, the only affordable place large enough to treat the vast amounts of pitchblende was a shed at the physics school that opened onto a large courtyard. The facilities here were no better than those of the first lab. The shed had been built as a dissecting room for the medical school, but was now in such a state of disrepair that for many years no one had even considered it fit for cadavers. An earthen floor, wooden plank walls, and a leaky glass roof housed cast-off kitchen tables, a rusty stove, and a forgotten blackboard which Pierre soon loved to use. Such was the laboratory where they had to conduct their sensitive

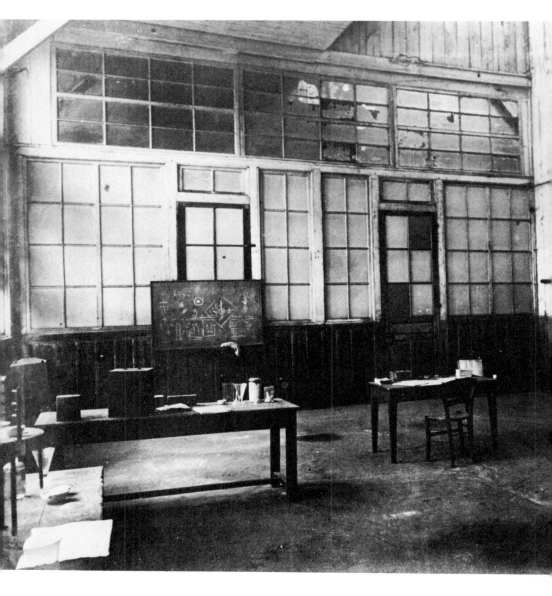

The laboratory in the shed at the
School of Physics, where Marie Curie and
her husband, Pierre, discovered radium.

research. A German chemist once came to visit them and wrote to a colleague that the lab was "a cross between a stable and a potato-cellar, and, if I had not seen the worktable with the chemical apparatus, I would have thought it a practical joke."

They had no problems with their material, however. The Curies were able to get several tons of waste pitchblende ore from a uranium mine in Bohemia. As the uranium which was used to color glass had already been extracted, they saved several months of work, as well as a lot of money.

Early in 1899, Marie heard a heavy horse-wagon clop down the street and stop outside the school. Still in her lab apron, Marie hurried outside to direct the carter, watching eagerly as the heavy sacks of pitchblende began to fill the courtyard. Unable to wait any longer, she ripped open one of the bags, scooped up a handful of the rich brown dust, still mixed with pine needles and other debris, and rushed into the lab. Her electrometer confirmed her guess. The waste pitchblende was more radioactive than the uranium that had been extracted from it. Polonium and radium were there.

Marie took about twenty kilos from the sack, sifted it, and then started to purify her first batch. She ground the ore, boiled it in vats set up in the courtyard, and filtered it until she had sufficiently small and concentrated samples of radioactive residue. Every day this tiny woman was at her labor, stirring the poisonous sludge with a heavy iron bar, carrying enormous jars of liquids and precipitates in and out of the shed. She worked outside over the cauldrons, carrying her chemicals indoors at the first drops of rain, even though water was just as likely to drip into the pots indoors as out. She and Pierre cooked their lunch and boiled the water for their tea over the laboratory fires, and when they needed a break, they strolled around the courtyard.

It was slow going. Samples were always being contaminated by coal dust or uncontrollable temperatures. Sometimes a careless movement knocked months of work into a puddle on the floor. Yet Marie never shrank from her chosen task, and gloried in her indescribable exhaustion every evening. She and Pierre thrived in the "untroubled quietness of this atmosphere of research and the excitement of actual progress with the hope of still better results." Despite the difficulties and occasional disappointments, they were very happy.

But within a year they had used up all their money. How would they live, or, more importantly to them, how would they buy more pitchblende? Pierre's teaching at the School of Physics didn't bring in much, and because of his shy and retiring nature he found it hard to get much-needed promotions. He turned down a lucrative offer in Geneva because a move would mean interrupting their quest, but took a better paying teaching job in Paris. Marie, too, went to teach in a girls' school in the nearby suburb of Sèvres. They secured their finances, but at the tremendous cost of time away from their research.

How discouraging to work so hard and see so little reward. After two years they still had not isolated radium. They were no longer working alone, however; other scientists came to help them in the lab. One of them, a chemist named André Debierne, discovered a third radioelement, actinium, in iron and rare earths by using the Curies' methods. But radium still hid.

Marie's letters to Poland remained cheerful, however. She let her family know about her teaching, about her success in making jam, and about Irène's new teeth, but rarely did she mention the work that took all her concentration and care. A letter to Bronya is typically dispassionate: "Our life is always the same. We work a lot. . . . During the whole of this year we have not been either to the theatre or a concert, and we have not paid one visit . . . I cannot complain. . . ."

While Marie carried on her purifications, slaving like a factory worker, Pierre devoted himself to studying the nature of radiation. He, along with other scientists who were now pursuing the problem in this and in other labs, determined that these elements gave off three types of radiation. Alpha rays were positively charged particles that could be stopped by a piece of paper. Negatively charged beta particles could penetrate an inch-thick piece of wood and cause a bad burn. The third radiation was the gamma ray, a wave of energy produced inside the atom when the alphas and betas were shot out. These were the deadliest rays, burning deep into any solid material, stopping only for a thick shield of lead.

Pierre observed these rays, but neither he nor Marie thought about the possible effect they might have on themselves. They attributed their chronic fatigue and low resistance to disease to overwork and undernourishment. A doctor friend, alarmed at their run-down condition, wrote to Pierre: "You scarcely eat, either of you. I have more than once seen Mme Curie nibbling two thin rounds of sausage and washing it down with a cup of tea . . . You don't spend enough time on your meals. . . . You musn't read while you eat, or talk physics. . . ."

The doctor meant well, but he was on the wrong track. Starvation alone couldn't account for the violent pains in Pierre's legs that forced him to spend days in bed, or for the badly burned and cracked fingers that made it difficult for either of them to hold a pen. These symptoms were the gift of radium. In discovering the element, the Curies were to be its first victims.

But no one knew that then. The Curies saw no reason to abandon their work. With the turn of the century, the vats disappeared from the courtyard. Inside, jars of ever more concentrated solutions lined the shelves. Marie never deviated from the principles of research which guided her work. She was always scrupulously careful of her measurements; she worked with samples that were as pure as possible, even if she had to refine vast quantities of material to get them; and she never formulated any general law until she was sure there were no exceptions to it. Her search for radium was based on procedures no less rigorous than those used by the police in a house-to-house search. There were no shortcuts. The patience she had learned as a governess and her innate stubbornness stood her in good stead.

In the meantime, however, the Curies discovered a new joy. Wrote Marie: "Sometimes we returned in the evening after dinner for another survey of our domain. Our precious products, for which we had no shelter, were arranged on tables and boards; from all sides we could see their slightly luminous silhouettes, and these gleamings, which seemed suspended in the darkness, stirred us with ever new emotion and enchantment."

The intensity of their work made them forget the physical and mental strains of their research, and ignore or endure their delays and failures. So absorbed were they in their new elements that Marie could say "we lived in a preoccupation as complete as that of a dream."

Early in the summer of 1900, Marie thought she had isolated radium. She couldn't refine the barium any farther, and she barely had enough of a sample to weigh. And when she did try to compute the new substance's atomic weight, the results were too low. There already was an element in that part of the periodic table. She'd made a mistake somewhere: she'd have to start all over and prepare another sample. Marie was to labor for two more years until she found success.

FAME

4

On a blustery day in March 1902, Marie threw on her coat, picked up a small test tube, and hurried over to the laboratory of her friend Eugène Demarçay. In the tube was a tenth of a gram of something that looked like table salt, but Marie was sure that this radium chloride was her purest sample yet.

Demarçay had been testing the chemical purity of Marie's products since 1898. He used a spectroscope, an instrument he invented to study the characteristic rainbow patterns (spectra) that each element shows when it is sparked by an electric current. Usually Demarçay could identify all the patterns he saw, but this time he found a line in the spectrum of Marie's sample that he had never seen before—a line that had to belong to the new element.

Encouraged by these results, Marie rushed back to the shed and began to compute the radium's atomic weight. Soon she was able to write in her notebook "Ra = 225.93." With the determination of this atomic weight, and with the new spectral line, "the chemical individuality of radium was completely established, and the reality of radioelements was a known fact about which there could be no further controversy." So wrote Marie, pride and self-satisfaction peeking through the unemotional prose.

She wasn't always so unemotional about her years of toil, however. Recognizing the backward conditions of her lab as the stuff legends are made of, she tried to balance the picture for posterity by admitting that ". . . this romantic element was not an advantage; it wore out our strength and delayed our accomplishment. With better means, the first five years of our work might have been reduced to two, and their tension lessened."

But those years of hard work, so exhausting that Pierre had even suggested they give up the search, had finally paid off. Marie *had* discovered something new and, in 1903, she wrote her dissertation and applied for her doctorate. Wearing a black dress bought just for the occasion, she stood quietly in a room well-stocked with family, friends, and students, and answered the questions the examination committee put to her. In an hour she had reviewed the progress of radioactivity to that day, and so impressed the professors that they added the praise *très honorable* to her degree.

Who could know more about the subject than Marie? True, the world knew of the Curies' work. Since Pierre had enthusiastically described their progress at a conference in 1900, chemists and physicists were eagerly learning all they could. No one else, however, had followed radium from the start, and knew it as well as a mother knows her child.

Marie was the first to determine that, in its pure state, radium was more than two million times more radioactive than the uranium it's found with. And she knew that radium had other characteristics just as wonderful as its strength. Without changing its appearance, and without using fuel or fire, a gram of radium could generate about one hundred calories of heat an hour, enough to melt its own weight in ice. Radium's rays bored through paper, tinted glass a lovely violet color, and gave a glow to materials which couldn't glow by themselves. Another property of radium was its generosity. Whatever came near it, even for a short time, became radioactive itself. Fifty years after she'd used them, some of Marie's notebooks and equipment from her lab were still too "hot" to touch, and had to be decontaminated before they could be used again.

One of radium's more fascinating talents was its ability to

burn and kill living tissue. Pierre once voluntarily exposed his arm to radiation for several hours. A burn-like lesion appeared on his skin that got progressively worse after the exposure and required several months to heal. Henri Becquerel, who carried a little tube of radium chloride in his vest pocket, was delighted and annoyed by a similar injury. Since the rays destroyed diseased tissue faster than healthy tissue, doctors experimented with treating certain skin disorders and cancers with small amounts of radium. This "Curie-therapy" was the first step toward modern radiation treatments for cancer.

Pierre published twenty-five papers about radioactivity between 1898 and 1904, all based on his experiments with the radium Marie was striving to isolate. Pierre was the first to describe induced radioactivity (how other substances become radioactive). He also investigated the spread of rays in the air, measured the heat radium gives off, and analyzed the radioactivity of mineral waters. Pierre even formulated a law to explain why the radiation from a particular sample grows weaker over a period of time.

One of his papers, done in collaboraton with Becquerel, studied the effects of radioactivity on mice and guinea pigs. The two men found that the radium gas changed the animals' immune systems, making them less able to fight disease, and altered their blood and lung tissue. Unfortunately, neither man chose to apply this information to humans. They knew that radium was dangerous; they even knew that lead was an effective shield against its radiations; yet they did nothing to protect themselves.

These steady publications meant that radium was fairly famous before Demarçay saw that new line in his spectroscope. They also meant that the Curies received many requests for information and help. Particularly pressing were letters from people who wanted to manufacture radium and supply the industrial and medical markets. These requests posed a problem for the Curies.

Pierre and Marie knew that, since they had invented the process for extracting radium, they could profit from it. They could ask anyone wanting to produce it to pay them for the information. The Curies carefully considered the tremendous wealth that would bring them. At last they would have enough money to build the laboratory of their dreams, to buy the materials they needed, to live comfortably, and to provide a great inheritance for Irène. All they had to do was consider themselves the owners of radium.

This was precisely what they morally could *not* do. They didn't even own the radium they had prepared—they considered that laboratory property. The Curies were members of a scientific generation that believed in the purity and disinterestedness of their work. Their obligation was to learn, explore, and publish their findings without any thought of profit or application. They labored only to find the truth, and if what they found could aid mankind in any way, then that was their reward.

It would have been contrary to the scientific spirit to expect financial gain from work undertaken with such an attitude. Nor were they willing to give up their science to concentrate on the business of producing radium, which they would have to do in order to make large amounts of money. That's why Pierre and Marie decided to publish completely the results of their work and to give all the details of the purification process to anyone who asked. In return for their advice, the Curies did obtain laboratory space and materials from some manufacturers. A radium industry had developed in France by the end of 1902, and soon after in the United States.

But even with more radium available, it was still very expensive. In fact, radium was the most valuable element in the world then, costing far more than gold. Only well-endowed laboratories could afford to buy it. For this reason the Curies shared their radioactive solutions and samples with other scientists. The possibility that other researchers using their own materials might beat them to an important breakthrough really didn't concern Pierre and Marie at all. For them, the only important thing was that the research be done and shared.

The Curies' work, and their incredibly powerful radioactive sources, started what Marie later described as a "general scientific movement." She was understating their impact. They had sparked a surge of interest and discovery throughout Europe and North America that changed the course of twentieth-century science. The concept of the atom as the smallest indivisible particle of matter, an idea inherited from the ancient Greeks, would no longer hold. Radium and polonium, with their subatomic activity, led scientists ultimately to the realization that one element could change into another and from that point to the development of atomic energy.

The Curies also changed the way physics was practiced. Radium was born into the twilight of classical physics, a discipline ruled by men with great practical skills. Marie herself was part of that tradition, having been taught that experimentation and measurement were the stepping stones to the truth. Based on their research techniques, physicists thought they had a good idea of the way elements behaved. But their old techniques couldn't help them explain the mysteries of Marie's glowing test tubes.

The challenge of finding new ways to attack these mysteries is what attracted research workers to the field. The quantity and quality of these scientists was such that between 1896 and 1911—from the discovery of X rays to the isolation of pure radium—radiochemical and radiophysical research moved at a phenomenal rate. For example, while Pierre and Marie toiled in their shed, other men in France, Germany, and Austria discovered almost simultaneously that some rays were deflected by magnetic fields. And, using the Curies' methods, about thirty other radioelements were found.

But the Curies' work had the greatest effect on a young physicist named Ernest Rutherford who wanted to know the *why* of radioactivity. Studying thorium and its gaseous emanation thoron, Rutherford and his colleague Frederick Soddy identified alpha rays as helium nuclei. Each time an atom of thorium threw off a helium nucleus it became an atom of thoron. This meant that radioelements destroy themselves by spontaneously transforming themselves into lighter elements. The more rapid the transformation, the more intense the radiation.

Marie later challenged Rutherford's claim to this theory, insisting that she and Pierre had suggested it several years earlier. But whoever thought of it first, Rutherford proved it. Pursuing his research in a lab so charged that even his assistant's breath was radioactive, Rutherford developed the first picture of the atom we recognize today. He suggested that the atom was basically empty, with tiny negatively charged electrons orbiting around a small but massive positively charged nucleus.

Building on Rutherford's work and guesses, other men like Max Planck and Niels Bohr extended the science of nuclear physics, using mathematical models and formulae instead of the traditional test tubes. But every new theory went back to the hypothesis that radiation is the release of the vast amounts of energy stored within the atom. Thanks to her solid training in mathematics as well as science, Marie was able to follow these theories and understand the world she had inspired.

It wasn't so easy to understand what was happening in their personal life, however. These years were the most exciting and productive for their work, yet Pierre and Marie were always tense, tired, and vaguely ill. Dark clouds, temporarily dispelled by the brilliance of their work, seemed to be creeping back into their skies.

The biggest and darkest was, as usual, lack of money. While their income allowed them to live in comparative comfort, much of their money and energy went into finding funding for their work. The Curies had chosen to live under this cloud, however, and suffered the consequences. They held fast to the "scientific dream" they had woven in Marie's garret, even when they saw it was turning into a nightmare. Simple needs and frugal habits helped them at home, but how could they cut back at the lab? They had to waste too much of their time and talent searching for funds and facilities. While some of the awards and prizes they won brought them money, many offered no material advantage. When he was awarded the Legion of Honor in 1903, Pierre declined it, saying, "I do not in the least feel the need of a decoration, but . . . I do feel the greatest need of a laboratory."

Pierre's ambivalent attitude toward advancing his career didn't help their finances either. His unconventional schooling deprived him of connections in the "old-boy network" that could easily have gotten him prestigious professorships and membership in the Academy of Science. What were his colleagues to make of a man who refused to court the favor of influential men in order to get a job, or who gave a gold medal to his tiny daughter for her to teethe on? Naturally they filled their ranks with men they understood, and Pierre was denied positions he both wanted and needed. Although he was quick to assure his friends that these constant rejections didn't trouble him personally, he soon stopped applying for anything. Instead of benefiting from his talent, Pierre became bitter and insecure.

To make ends meet, the Curies were forced into more teaching. They devoted as much energy to this as to the lab. Marie continued at Sèvres, devising for her hardworking students ever more complicated problems to solve. Pierre, too, introduced parctical exercises into his curricula. He didn't believe that anyone could learn science just from books and lectures, and so he made up innovative experiments and demonstrations for his classes.

Personal troubles in those years took an additional toll on the couple. Marie was emotionally and physically devastated by the death of her father in 1902. She had always felt very guilty about "abandoning" him to live in France, and she was particularly horrified at not having arrived in Warsaw in time to comfort him before he died.

Illness still dogged the Curies, too. Pierre's attacks of what he called rheumatism became more severe and more frequent, and he took to dosing himself with strychnine for the pain. He and Marie attributed his aches and pains to the strains and stresses of teaching coupled with the frustration of not being able to spend more time in the lab. Both of them still refused to consider that their beloved radium might be a cause of Pierre's suffering.

And by now Marie was sick, too. In 1903, she recorded in her account book that she had lost fifteen pounds while working in the shed, and she often felt weak and dizzy. When she became pregnant for the second time, she still went to the lab every day, exposing herself and the baby to extraordinarily high doses of radiation. Her general weakness and morning sickness conspired to make her feel terrible, yet she insisted she was fit and strong. To prove it, she kept up her regimen of physical exercise and even took a long bike trip in the late summer. But she was wrong about her strength. Her child was born prematurely and died just a few hours after birth. No one ever found any direct evidence for the cause of the miscarriage.

Marie lost what was left of her vitality after this misfortune. She wrote to her sister Bronya that she was "absolutely desolate and cannot be consoled." The loss of her father and baby within a year, on top of the strain of the life she had been living for the past ten years, pushed Marie into a nervous collapse. She began to walk in her sleep, and confessed to Pierre that all she wanted to do was eat, sleep, and think of nothing. Her husband, ever mindful of their mission, prescribed more work as an antidote to too much introspection.

That was not what Marie needed at all. She had worked hard for the last twenty years, supporting herself, earning her education, doing brilliant and exhausting research. She realized, perhaps for the first time, that she had never been young. When had she last had the luxury of doing something for the sheer fun of it? Even her adored Pierre came hand in hand with work. Much of Marie's torment at this time was not physical, but mental. She was having what we today would call an identity crisis, questioning the road she had taken, and wondering what she had missed.

Marie was severely depressed, and functioned as mechanically and unemotionally as a robot.

The Curies' life together was not always so gloomy. They had their share of satisfactions that made their circumstances tolerable. Certainly their work provided real pleasure. Pierre was especially happy when he could invent a new apparatus for an experiment—the more delicate, the better. And the close-knit circle of scientists and students who worked with them supplied good companionship as well as new ideas and interpretations for experiments. Marie particularly enjoyed the brainstorming sessions in the lab. Pierre would stand at the blackboard, illustrating some idea he had, while the others offered their thoughts in an "atmosphere of peace and contemplation." One of their colleagues remembered that in these meetings Pierre would have the ingenious ideas and see the odd angles to a problem, but that it was Marie's dogged persistence that carried these theories to their logical conclusions.

They carried their simple and serious laboratory manner home with them. Their house was quiet and orderly. Pierre and Marie rarely went out in the evening, preferring to sit at home in their bathrobes and slippers, poring over the latest physics journals. Marie did very little entertaining except for birthday parties. Far more pleasant for her was sitting outside in the garden on a sunny Sunday, talking shop and devising new experiments with the colleagues who were also their neighbors, while the children played tag on the grass.

Sometimes they were forced to go out. Pierre and Marie had to attend many scientific meetings, lectures, and receptions. They would put on evening dress—Pierre's shiny black suit and Marie's black lace gown that she had altered to fit every occasion—and endure the event. Pierre got through these ordeals by calculating how many labs he could equip for the price of the jewels he saw on the ladies' necks. But he had no games to help him with the fame that overwhelmed them when, in 1903, they were awarded the Nobel Prize for discovering radium.

Suddenly radium became all the rage. In a world grown used to miracles, this element captured the imaginations of laypeople and scientists alike. In the nineteenth century people had heard the secrets of their hearts for the first time with the invention of the stethoscope, seen images of themselves reproduced by cameras, copper plates, and the genius of a man named Louis Daguerre. Louis Braille had helped the blind to read, and Louis Pasteur had destroyed the terrors of rabies and the germs in raw milk. Electric lamps now lit up the cities, and someone named Louis Lumière was actually making moving pictures. Adding machines, telephones, gyroscopes, phosphorous matches—even rayon—were products of that century's vision. But in 1903 nothing was as magical or as exciting as the glowing substance of radium.

It was not only the tiny amount of radium that had the world so excited. The furor had at least as much to do with the persistence of its discoverer and the extreme conditions under which she worked. The press were quick to recognize what good copy Marie Curie would make. A woman with a small child, doing a man's work on workman's hours in a ramshackle shed in a backyard, laboring for four years to get what she wanted—Marie's story had all the trappings of a heroic legend. She, and of course Pierre, became overnight celebrities.

Now every day the mail brought hundreds of requests for interviews, articles, and autographs. Actors spoofed the Curies in cabaret acts. Pierre complained that journalists and photographers pursued them everywhere, publishing conversations be-

Following the discovery
of radium, the Curies
continued to spend many
hours together in the lab
studying the new element.

tween Irène and her nurse, and joked ruefully that they even interviewed the family's black and white cat. Marie was amazed at the sonnets written to radium, amused at the strange letters they got from spirits, mediums, and philosophers, and astonished by one American's offer to name a racehorse after her.

But while the public may have appreciated the discoverers, they showed little understanding of their discovery. Inventors, doctors, and scientists all had ideas for using the miraculous element, but one of the odder proposals came from an American named Loïe Fuller. Loïe had been a dancer with Buffalo Bill's Wild West Show, and was now a star of the Folies-Bergère. Her trademark was the unusual lighting she used in her choreography. Radium, she decided, would be just the thing to give her butterfly costume's wings an unearthly glow, and she wrote the Curies to find out how to do it.

Politely but firmly, Pierre and Marie explained to Loïe the impracticality of her idea. She was so touched by the kindness of their reply that she offered to come and dance for them in their home. One morning the dancer arrived at the Curie door with costumes, scenery, and an army of electricians. Rooms were closed off, the family was quarantined in the parlor, and all day the house clanged and buzzed with the efforts of the crew. By evening the dining room had been transformed into a magical garden, and Loïe danced for the dumfounded couple under hundreds of twinkling fairy lights. In spite of what must have been a startling experience for them, their acquaintance with Loïe blossomed into a friendship that lasted many years.

For Marie, however, already sorely tried by illness, pregnancy, and overwork, the Nobel Prize "had all the effects of a disaster." Their family and professional lives were nearly destroyed by all the hub-bub that followed the Nobel announcement. While Marie knew that people generally meant well by all their clamoring, she wished they would stop and think about how it was wasting her time.

And now she had another strain to add to her load. Early in 1904, before they could go to Sweden to collect their prize, Marie realized she was pregnant again. Terrified of another accident, this time she took better care of herself. She cut out her teaching, indulged her cravings (especially for caviar), rested more, and summoned Bronya to be with her. But she wouldn't allow herself to get excited about the baby, crying once: "Why am I bringing this creature into the world? Existence is too hard, too barren. We ought not inflict it on innocent ones."

Eve Denise Curie was born in December of that year, perfect and healthy. Her mother improved, too, with enforced rest and a monitored diet. The troubles of the earlier months faded, and by early spring Marie had come to terms with herself and her life. She understood that, for her and Pierre, life was work, and that she had made the only choices she could. The turmoil was over and never to be relived, or even referred to.

They were not ready to make the trip to Sweden until June 1905. Even then, neither Curie was very strong. An observer at the ceremony wrote that when Pierre got up to make his acceptance speech, he "rose to glory with the spirit of a whipped dog."

Besides the tribute of their fellow scientists, the Nobel Prize brought the Curies about seventy thousand gold francs. The Curies didn't refuse this money, planning to use it to buy more time and equipment for research. It also gave them a chance to indulge themselves a bit. After putting most of the money into a bank account, Pierre and Marie earmarked the rest for pet projects. A sizable sum went to the tuberculosis hospital Bronya and her husband were building in Poland, and cash gifts went to other relatives. They sent money for subscriptions to scientific journals and to the underground Polish liberation movement. The Curies set up scholarships for their laboratory. Marie wired money to a former teacher in Warsaw so that the old woman could return to visit her native France. A final indulgence was spending money on their house: Marie chose new wallpaper for one room and ordered the installation of a modern bathroom.

It was typical of them that they didn't think to buy a bigger house, take a trip, buy jewels, or even a new hat. No matter that they were now the most famous couple in the world. They remained true to themselves and their dreams.

ALONE

5

In many ways life improved for the Curies after the Nobel Prize. Other awards and honors followed, and some of their financial troubles seemed over. The French government finally recognized Pierre's fame and in 1904 created a new chair of physics at the Sorbonne just for him. Pierre refused the post until he got a written promise of a place to work as well as teach. This assurance came with an offer to name Marie the chief of the new lab. Although this was exactly the work she'd been doing for years, Marie now had a title and, better yet, a salary.

Promises and professorships were all very fine, but in reality it was two years before they had even a couple of spare rooms at the Sorbonne. In the meantime the Curies maintained their shed at the School of Physics and Chemistry. Marie still taught at Sèvres, enjoying the change of pace, colleagues, and atmosphere; for two days a week she wasn't breathing radioactive air. And Pierre never stopped looking for better facilities for them. He felt strongly enough about their needs to write to a potential patron that ". . . it is of capital importance for us to live with our children where we work. Children and a laboratory exact the constant presence of those who take care of them. . . . Life is very difficult when the home and the laboratory are far from each other."

Their search for a lab had recently taken on a new urgency. By 1905 Pierre was always ill and fatigued. Each day he became more absentminded, and often seemed to be living in his own world. When Marie once asked him how he'd enjoyed his dinner, he looked up at her in astonishment. "Did I eat a beefsteak?" he asked, and then murmured, "It's quite possible."

Marie lived in fear and dread. What would happen to him? Pierre could neither reassure her nor quiet her unease because he didn't know what was wrong, either. All he could do was remind her that "whatever happens, even if one has to go on like a body without a soul, one must work just the same."

Things were looking better in the late winter of 1906 when their rooms at the Sorbonne were finally ready. Regretfully they packed to leave the old shed where they had "known such happy workdays, despite their attendant difficulties." But they both knew that more comfortable and productive days lay ahead.

Easter came late that year, and the four Curies spent the holiday in the country. Unusually warm weather forced the flowers and birds out into the early spring sunlight. The family cycled, picnicked, and played in the grass. While Pierre and Marie rested under a tree, Irène ran after butterflies with a net that was taller than she was, and little Eve toddled after her. They all felt it was the start of a new life together, sweet and satisfying.

Pierre returned to Paris to attend a dinner meeting of a scientific society on Wednesday, April 18. He boarded the train carrying only the things he loved best—his papers and a bunch of wild flowers. Marie and the girls were to follow the next day.

The weather changed overnight, and Thursday dawned wet and miserable. Pierre, bundled into his coat and hat, set off for an appointment in Paris. Head down under his big black umbrella, his

Marie and Pierre were photographed as they set off on a bicycle excursion in 1906, shortly before Pierre's death.

mind on last night's meeting, he didn't hear the people shouting at him to watch where he was going. When he did look up it was too late. A heavy horse-drawn wagon was almost upon him. Pierre was momentarily paralyzed with shock, then he lifted his arm as if to grab onto the horse's reins as it reared before him, but he lost his balance and slipped onto the shiny pavement. The wheels rolled over him, crushing his skull in fifteen or sixteen places. Death, mercifully, was instantaneous.

At six that evening Marie, happy to be home again and eagerly anticipating a return to their normal routine, turned the key in the lock. She was surprised to see her old teacher, Paul Appell, in the living room with her father-in-law. No one spoke. Marie's eyes traveled from the two men to the bowl of flowers Pierre had placed on the bookshelf.

"Pierre is dead? Really dead?" Grief-stricken as she was, Marie did her mourning privately. Her remarkable self-control brought her through the nightmare days that followed the accident, protecting her with an invisible wall of silence. But this wall, which shielded her from the public and the press, also shut her off from the comfort of the people she was close to. And it was a wall she never completely tore down.

Old Dr. Curie (who upon hearing the news could only mutter "What was he thinking of this time?"), Pierre's brother Jacques, and the Sklodowskas helped Marie through the simple funeral at Sceaux. But she could not speak of her misery even to them. Lost and alone in her grief, she found a gray notebook on the shelf and began to write.

In those pages, the only diary she ever kept, Marie fixed for all time the details of the tragedy and of their life together. In shaking handwriting she poured out love letters to Pierre, describing how "sweet and serene" he looked, "lost in a dream from which you cannot get out." After the funeral she wrote: "Everything is over, Pierre is sleeping his last sleep beneath the earth; it is the end of everything, everything, everything."

For weeks afterward she jumped at the sound of the front door slamming, believing for a moment that she would hear Pierre's foot on the step. She tried to carry on as usual. After she told the children about his death, she never mentioned Pierre to them again. She and Jacques went back to work—they even visited the lab the day after the funeral—but she said, "I felt the impossibility of going on."

Marie had lost a husband, a colleague, and a friend. It takes a long time to comprehend and accept the extent of such a loss. On May 7 she wrote in her diary:

> My Pierre, I think of you all the time, my head is bursting with the thought of you, and my reason fails. I can't understand that I have to live without you and that I can't smile at my dear life's companion. The trees have been in leaf two days now and the garden is beautiful. This morning I was admiring the children in it. I thought how beautiful you would have thought them and that you would have called me to show me that the periwinkles and narcissus were out . . .

In June, the night before her sister Bronya was to return to Poland, Marie called her to her room. Although the night was hot, a fire blazed in the grate. Without a word Marie took from a drawer a pair of shears and a rumpled brown paper parcel. The package contained the clothes Pierre had worn when he died, now stiff and dirty, stained with blood and bits of flesh. Marie hugged and kissed the grisly garments until Bronya pulled them away from her and, finding a second pair of scissors, started to cut up the clothes and throw them in the fire. The two sisters worked in silence until everything, even the towel they wiped their hands on, was consumed by flames. Only then did Marie break down, sobbing out her anguish in her sister's arms, asking over and over "How am I to live?"

But in the morning she was calm again, and better able to address the practical aspects of her terrible question. The public had rallied to the cause of the thirty-nine-year-old widow, sending offers of pensions and charitable subscriptions along with their condolences and eulogies. While Marie was gratifed by these outpourings, believing they showed her husband's death was a national as well as personal tragedy, she stubbornly refused all charity. She was young and strong and could earn a living for her family. She would go on working, as Pierre had insisted she do.

Within two weeks of Pierre's death, Marie had a job that guaranteed a salary of ten thousand francs a year plus a lab. It was a post she was ideally suited for, and there was no one better qualified for it. The University hired Marie to take over Pierre's position, and she became the first woman professor at the Sorbonne.

Here was a chance for her to enhance the Curie name while proving herself the equal of the men she would have to work with. Marie sent Irène and Eve to the country for the summer and threw herself into researching, writing, and polishing her lectures. It all had to be perfect by the opening of the fall term when the world's attention would be focused on the debut of the grieving Nobel laureate whose tragic story had captured its heart.

For weeks before the first lecture Marie was the darling of the press. One newspaper saw her appointment as a victory for feminism. "How can men be superior if women teach them?" asked the editor. "I tell you, the time is near when women will become human beings." Other papers speculated about whether Madame Curie would honor the ancient Sorbonne tradition of praising one's predecessor. What would she say about Pierre?

On a raw November day, thirteen years after she had entered as a hopeful student, Marie arrived at the Sorbonne to teach her first class. Her lecture was scheduled for 1:30, but by noon the noisy mob gathered outside the hall was so large that the doors were opened early to let them all scramble for seats. Students were in the minority that day. Marie, the woman who quaked when addressing schoolgirls, had an audience of professors, journalists, socialites, and tourists.

Just before 1:30 the door near the desk opened and Marie, thin and wan in her old black dress, slipped into the room and grasped the podium. With a quick half-bow to the assembly, she shuffled her papers and in clear, well-modulated tones began: "When we consider the progress which has taken place in physics during the last ten years, we are surprised at the change in our ideas concerning electricity and matter. . . ."

She continued this way for the next hour, simply picking up the course where Pierre had left it. The spectators were amazed. They had expected tears and tributes; instead they got a serious scientific lecture that made no concession to the laypersons in the crowd, but was geared to the needs of the handful of physics students present. Only those sitting in the front of the hall saw how pale she was or how her lips trembled, and glimpsed the tremendous emotion that all but overwhelmed her. Marie made her point. She was not to be pitied; she did not need charity; she would carry on as well as or perhaps better than Pierre. She was qualified to accomplish his dream of building a great laboratory for the study of radioactivity and the training of a new generation of scientists.

Such an attitude only enhanced her reputation and her legend. Andrew Carnegie, the American millionaire, was so impressed with her pluck that he endowed her lab with fifty thousand dollars in gold bonds. The income financed scholarships for advanced students and scientists, and one of the first went to her nephew Maurice Curie. Best of all, Carnegie specified in his grant that "Mme. Curie's wishes should be respected," tactfully telling the Sorbonne who was really in charge.

With her career and lab secure, Marie could now turn some of her attention to her children. While she made it clear that her "children's education was only a part of my duties, my profes-

sional occupations taking most of my time," she still had to face their care and nurturing, and reconcile their needs with her career. "Well," she wrote, "it has not been easy; it required a great deal of decision and self-sacrifice."

Marie's goal was to give her girls the freedom to mold their own futures. Irène and Eve received no religious training, although they were never kept from joining any church. They spoke Polish and French, and from an early age were encouraged to explore Paris by themselves to learn independence. Mindful of their physical development, Marie installed a jungle gym in the backyard, complete with swings, rings, and ropes, where the girls played every day. They also took daily walks, and learned to swim, ride, and cycle. Irène and Eve grew up fearless and fit.

Formal schooling was more of a problem. Marie was unhappy with the French lycées that kept students working at their desks in school and at home for too much of the day. She was also disappointed with the unimaginative science curricula. So together with several sympathetic colleagues she set up a cooperative school for their children. The professors taught their specialties to the students, who spent a good part of the day traveling from one scholar to another.

Marie, of course, taught science, developing technique while explaining theory. Her pupils remembered her as a kind and patient teacher who was good at posing mind-stretching questions. Eve recalled one class about heating and cooling in particular.

"What can I do to keep the liquid in this pan hot?" asked Marie.

Instantly small hands waved about her. "Isolate it." "Wrap it in wool." "Put it in a box."

Marie with her daughters,
Eve (left) and Irène.

Their teacher considered each suggestion gravely, then smiled gently and said: "I would first of all put the lid on," before sending them out to play.

The cooperative experiment lasted about three years, finally falling victim to scheduling problems. Despite a heavy scientific bent to the program, the students were well prepared to rejoin traditional schools. They had learned two important lessons: to think for themselves and to enjoy hard work. The only thing they didn't learn was social grace. In their very limited circle there was little opportunity to meet and converse with strangers.

By this time Marie had moved to Sceaux so that the girls could have fresh air. Although she now commuted an hour to work, Marie was glad Irène could have her own garden, and Eve could adopt every animal that wandered through the yard. Grandfather Curie and a distant cousin of Marie's cared for the children during the day. Marie saw them at dinner, after a long day at the lab. Then she retired to her room to spend half the night sitting on the floor, surrounded by papers, studying and writing.

It wasn't much time in which to know her children. The two girls were equally gifted, but in different ways. Irène was just the sort of child you might expect the Curies to produce. She loved physics, chemistry, and mathematics. Introverted and shy, she seemed unaware and uncaring of others, and always had great difficulties in social situations. Marie was very proud of her, and pages of her autobiography glow with references to "my daughter Irène."

Marie wrote only brief sentences about "my other daughter," however. Eve, seven years Irène's junior, was pretty, musical, and charming. Strangers warmed to her as they could not to her sister or mother. Poise and humor helped Eve hide her misery at being the misfit in the family. She knew she was excluded from the emotional and intellectual bond the other two shared. Openly admitting that her childhood was not happy, Eve nevertheless was the one who wrote the famous and adoring biography of her mother, *Madame Curie.*

Her children and her work saved Marie's sanity during the early years of her widowhood, and she guarded both jealously. She drove herself harder than ever, determined to forget her sorrow in the laboratory Pierre never had. Her devotion and perseverance turned her into more than a celebrity with a tragic past. In these years before the first world war Marie became a leading figure in the international scientific community, a recognized expert in a fraternity of experts.

What was she working on at the time? Still a positivist at heart, Marie set herself the task of isolating pure radium and polonium in order to prove their existence without a doubt both to herself and other chemists; until then she had prepared only highly concentrated salts. This was just the kind of tedious, time-consuming, and exacting work she was so good at. Within one year she had prepared a sample of radium chloride so pure she was able to recalculate radium's atomic weight, and three years later she saw for the first time the shiny white metal itself. The isolation process she used was so difficult and complicated, involving such a risk of losing radium, that it has never been repeated. Nor could Marie afford to keep it in this state; it was more useful in compound.

While she couldn't isolate polonium, she was able to prepare some highly concentrated compounds in order to refute a German scientist who claimed to have discovered a new radioelement. Skeptical of his report, Marie was convinced he had merely rediscovered polonium. She repeated his research, and rebutted his conclusions in German journals to show the hapless man's errors to his countrymen as well as his colleagues.

In 1908 she developed and gave the world's first course in radioactivity at the Sorbonne. That year also saw the publication of a six-hundred-page-volume of the *Works of Pierre Curie*. For the previous two years Marie had patiently and painfully collected, arranged, and edited her husband's notes and articles to create a permanent memorial to his genius.

Her other major scientific project during these years was

determining an internationally acceptable unit of measurement for radium. Such a standard is essential for successful and consistent experiments and therapy. However, because radium occurs in such small amounts, conventional measures are useless. Marie proposed measuring the radiation instead of the radium, and devised a unit called the Curie, the quantity of emanation from one gram of radium in one second. She herself prepared the first standard against which all others would be adjusted.

But was anything really new coming out of her laboratory? By 1910, a few scientists were beginning to think not. Even Ernest Rutherford, who never denied his debt to her work, questioned the originality of her experiments and the need for the tedious tasks she was forever undertaking. When her thousand page *Treatise on Radioactivity* appeared in print, Rutherford complained that it was "very heavy and very long . . . with very little critical discussion." As if to soften the blow, he added: "The poor woman has labored tremendously."

What Rutherford failed to realize was that the *Treatise* was a concrete expression of Marie's personality and her positivism. Like her, the book was thorough, correct, and dispassionate. She explained the facts, justified her work and her methods, and made sure she got proper credit in the pages of her encyclopedia.

Unfortunately, her desire for recognition and honor blinded her to the dark side of celebrity—envy and gossip. Had she seen those, she would never have opened herself to the two events, one public and one private, that ruined her health and peace of mind in 1911.

When Marie accepted the nomination to the vacant chair at the French Academy of Science, an association of the country's most distinguished scientists, she saw both the honor her adopted country was offering her and the painful politicking she would have to do in order to actually win the seat. She didn't see the envy of her colleagues or fully appreciate the extent of their prejudice against women, even when one Academy member thundered to the press that "Women cannot be members of the Institute of France!"

While Marie made her courtesy calls on the men who would decide on her membership, her opponents prepared a whispering campaign against her. Suddenly she found herself accused of being the "foreign woman" who had come to France only to seize the honors and positions that by rights belonged to French *men*.

She missed election to the Academy by two votes. Although she insisted that the rejection didn't bother her and refused the consolations of students and friends, Marie had to admit she had misjudged her standing among her peers, and to realize that her sex was still very much a barrier to equality. She also learned never to trust the press, or a world in which she was a hero one day and a villain the next.

Before the year was out she had another reason for hating the press. Shortly after her Academy defeat a newspaper published some private letters Marie had written to her friend and co-worker Paul Langevin.

A brilliant physicist in his own right, Langevin was charming, handsome, and unhappily married. Marie, now widowed five years, was growing more beautiful with age and the melancholy strength which shaped her expression. Their attraction and affection was mutual and deep. Marie naively assumed that none of their friends would notice, even though she suddenly started wearing white dresses instead of her usual solemn black, and one night even put flowers in her hair. Of course people noticed. Those who were genuinely fond of her were happy for the change; those who weren't, gossiped.

The result was a spectacular scandal that dragged the Curie name through the journalistic mud for several weeks. Marie was called a homewrecker (even though the Langevins were already separated) and an immoral foreigner. Crowds used to gather in front of her house to harass her, throw stones, or just stare. Marie and the girls were prisoners in their own home, afraid to risk the wrath of the public.

Although at one point the situation became so explosive that Langevin challenged a particularly vicious reporter to an abortive duel, the affair was out of the papers in a few months. Langevin worked out an uneasy but diplomatic reconciliation with his wife and left the lab, taking with him Marie's chances for happiness and companionship. While her only comment on the scandal was a terse entry in her account book—"Expenses L. affair, 378 francs"—Marie was now in a state of collapse, having lost two fond hopes in one year.

There was one consolation for the terrible year, however. On November 8, 1911, at the height of the scandal, Marie received a telegram awarding her the Nobel Prize for chemistry. The prize was for her isolation of pure radium, but since she had broken no new ground in doing so, it's far more likely that the award was really given as a response to Marie's personal and political troubles. Her scientific associates were assuring her that, no matter what the French might think, the world respected her and her work.

Marie traveled to Stockholm with Bronya and Irène to collect the prize. In her acceptance speech she acknowledged the honor both as a tribute to her work and as "homage to Pierre Curie." The trip was too much for her, however and, on December 29, she was taken to the hospital on a stretcher.

Marie swore she was suffering from "the result of all the cares devolving on me;" her body had rebelled against stress this way before. But her doctors disagreed with her, diagnosing a kidney condition which they cured with surgery.

Her recuperation took many months. She stayed with friends in France and England, traveling under assumed names to protect her anonymity. She was terrified lest the press find out about her illness and plaster her name all over their front pages again.

Marie recovered from her operation, but she never recovered from her five years alone in the spotlight. She withdrew into herself as a defense against more notoriety. Soon she had a reputation for being icy, aloof, and unhelpful, a reputation she never bothered to contradict. And forever after, if a stranger approached her on the street and eagerly asked, "Aren't you Marie Curie?" she would turn aside, trembling, and murmur "No, you must be mistaken."

MOVING
OUT

6

The future looked brighter in the new year. Marie's dream of a great laboratory came true. In fact, she found herself in charge of two labs, one in Paris and one in Warsaw.

After organizing its activities from afar, Marie traveled to Warsaw in 1913 for the official opening of the lab. While there, Marie had the thrill of delivering her first scientific lecture in Polish in the museum housing the lab where she had discovered her vocation twenty years earlier. Her trip was sweetened by two other events. One was that the Russian officials completely ignored both her visit and the lab, too chagrined at this palpably Polish achievement to try to Russianize it. The other occurred at a banquet in Marie's honor. At one of the tables Marie caught sight of a tiny old lady in black and impulsively left her seat on the dais and ran to embrace her. She was the principal of Marie's grammar school, who had followed her pupil's career with pride and admiration, and who was overwhelmed at Marie's public demonstration of love and esteem.

The new Polish lab, modest as it was, reminded the directors at the Sorbonne that they still hadn't built the lab they'd promised Pierre in 1904. If they wanted to keep his widow in France they would have to provide facilities comparable to Poland's. They established a two part Radium Institute: the Pasteur Laboratory would study the biological and medical applications of radioactivity in one building; and the Curie Laboratory would investigate the physical and chemical properties of radioelements in a building across the courtyard. Marie was to be in charge of this lab and, best of all, the new street leading to the Institute would be called rue Pierre Curie.

Marie threw herself into the directorship with all the energy and enthusiasm of one who had been waiting a long time for her big chance. She supervised the building of the "Curie Pavilion," insisting on such unheard of amenities as an elevator, big windows, and a garden in the central courtyard. Every day the little figure in black would inspect the site, consult with the carpenters, and advise the architects. Everything had to be perfect.

During the construction Marie got an anguished call from a former assistant at the School of Physics and Chemistry. Her old shed was about to be demolished to make room for more classroom space. Marie paid a final visit that same day. The first thing she saw when she entered the room was the old blackboard, still covered with Pierre's handwriting. For an instant she stood there, expecting him to come from behind the board and pick up the experiment he had been outlining. The sensation and memories were so painful that Marie had to leave quickly. In the new building there would be no ghosts.

Finally on July 31, 1914, Marie stood before the doors of the Curie Pavilion. Equipment was in place, the big windows sparkled in the sunlight, the flowers she had planted bloomed in the courtyard. Her dream had come true. In a week, she thought, she and her students would be hard at work in those rooms, enjoying the great adventure of scientific pursuit.

But within a week only Marie and an ailing mechanic wandered through the empty halls. Europe was at war.

Irène and Eve were spending the summer in the country. Marie sent them news each day about the mobilization of the army and conditions in Paris. She ended one letter to Irène with the admonition that "You and I must try to make ourselves useful." But when and how would that be?

Marie knew she had to stay in Paris and guard her laboratory, figuring the Germans wouldn't dare plunder it if she were there. She also wanted to stay as an example of courage and calm in the face of the panic and mass evacuation that was sweeping the capital city; she even allowed her children to rejoin her as further proof that she was not afraid.

The only thing she felt did need special protection was her radium. On a hot day in August she packed the precious sample in a leaden suitcase that, at twenty kilos, was too heavy for her to lift. An assistant drove her to the station and helped her onto a train packed with tearful mothers and screaming children fleeing the city. Slowly the train wound itself to Bordeaux. From the windows Marie could see the roads clogged with private vehicles, all carrying their owners to the comparative safety of the countryside. Thanks to a kind stranger she was able to get the radium into a Bordeaux bank vault, find food and lodging and, against all advice, return on the next morning's train to Paris. People thought she was mad. Marie, however, kept explaining that Paris was in no danger, and urged others to come back with her to help their country as they could.

Once home, she stopped at her apartment only long enough to wash and eat, and then hurried off to volunteer her help. Marie was among the first to realize several things about this war: that it would be long; that it would be unlike any previous war; and that it would produce vast numbers of wounded. She also admitted sadly that her own scientific work would be of little direct benefit to the war effort.

But she did have a skill she could put to use, and for once she did not hesitate to apply her science to a practical purpose. Marie proposed to bring X rays, now only in limited use in civilian hospitals, to the battlefields. That way the wounded could be treated without the agony of a long ride in a clattering ambulance to the nearest hospital. She would bring medical care closer to the soldiers, not the other way around.

Marie's plan had two major hurdles to jump. First was equipment. Few hospitals had X-ray apparatus in 1914. She had to borrow machines from schools and labs, and beg for funds to buy more. Marie also approached wealthy citizens for donations of cars and cash to get her mobile units rolling.

Her second problem was manpower. She would have trouble finding capable volunteers to run the apparatus once most of the able-bodied men—even the students and scientists—were drafted. Marie decided to learn to do it all herself so that she could train others and make sure her service was totally self-sufficient. Systematically, and with typical thoroughness, Marie perfected her X-ray techniques and pored over medical books in order to know what she was photographing. She also learned to drive and repair a car, for there was no one else to do it.

Marie started several permanent X-ray stations around Paris in September 1914. She soon saw that the service would have to move to the ever-changing battlefields in order to be truly useful. The following month, when seventeen-year-old Irène arrived to help her mother, the first "Radiologic Car" was ready to go. It was simply a touring car fitted with an X-ray machine run by a dynamo that worked off the engine, photographic equipment, and a few screens and gloves to protect the operators from overexposure to the rays. Soon Marie had readied twenty such cars and, by learning to harass officials and generals for the clearances and passes she needed, was able to send units to several sites at once.

Marie herself traveled in a Renault truck with a French flag painted on one side and a huge red cross on the other. Uniformed in a dusty brown coat and hat, she carried only her old leather briefcase and her big man's wallet holding her dearest possessions: her passes; photographs of herself, her father, and two of her mother; and two packets of seeds that she meant to plant at the Institute as soon as things got quieter. Marie would drive her truck to the field hospital closest to the fighting. As soon as she put on the brake she would jump out and begin dragging the heavy equipment into the hospital. She and Irene would improvise a darkroom with blankets and blackout curtains, set up the machines, and within the hour start to X ray the terrible parade of the wounded. The women worked for hours on end. They listed their cases in a special notebook that not only recorded their patients but also helped blunt the horror of what they saw: "Bullet in forearm," "Ball shrapnel in right hand," "Examination of cranium, rifle bullet in central region."

The car stayed as long as there were wounded. Marie sometimes stayed a little longer to set up a more permanent installation if she felt it necessary. In two years she had organized two hundred such units throughout France and Belgium. The tiny shabby lady and her young daughter lived like soldiers, toiling in these primitive places tirelessly, comforting soldiers, assisting doctors, lending extra hands to volunteer nurses. At one place they worked right alongside the King and Queen of Belgium, who also served as volunteers.

It was an exhausting, dangerous life, plagued always with the problems of finding food, lodging, and passable roads. Marie endured it all philosophically; as she said: "Things always ended in arranging themselves." Not even a car accident could upset her. When she once drove the truck into a ditch, she ignored her own and the car's injuries. Her only concern was that the equipment might be smashed. In her efforts to ease the sufferings of others, Marie's shyness, introspection, and self-preoccupation disappeared.

As the war dragged on, and all her original technicians had been called into uniform, Marie had to find a new generation of X-ray operators. She decided to use a hitherto untapped resource—women. In 1916 she and Irène began a training course at the Radium Institute. One hundred and fifty women from all backgrounds—farmgirls, clerks, and nurses—went through the class. Marie excluded only those who were too clumsy, too stupid, or too afraid. The women learned basic mathematics, physics, and anatomy, and upon "graduation" manned the X-ray cars and installations. By November 1918 together with Marie, they had treated more than one million wounded.

Whatever satisfaction Marie found in her labor was more than balanced by the misery she saw. In her autobiography she described how she felt about the war:

> I can never forget the terrible impression of all that destruction of human life and health. To hate the very idea of war, it ought to be sufficient to see once what I have seen so many times, all through those years: men and boys brought to the advanced ambulance in a mixture of mud and blood, many of them dying of their injuries, many others recovering but slowly through months of pain and suffering . . .

Marie Curie was not always at the Front. She wanted to use her new lab, and get things ready for when the war was over. With the help of Irène and her assistant, she arranged and rearranged the heavy equipment and jars of chemicals. But her main concern at that time was more for landscaping than for laboratories. Believing that tired eyes need to look at fresh leaves, she planted a few lime trees, some plane trees, and planned flower beds and rose gardens. She fondly recalled that "the first day of bombardment of Paris with the big German gun, we had gone in the early morning, to the flower market, and spent all that day busy with our plantation, while a few shells fell in the vicinity."

Once it became clear that Paris wouldn't fall, Marie brought her radium back from Bordeaux. It wasn't used for research now, but for medicine. Each week small amounts of radiation were drawn from the sample, sealed in thin glass tubes and sent to hospitals where doctors placed them directly in patients' bodies to treat scar tissue and joint diseases.

Marie helped France's war effort in one other way. She

bought war bonds with her Nobel Prize money. She offered her gold medals as well, but the French government refused to let her melt them down. Marie checked first with Irène before giving up her money, not wanting to "commit such nonsense" without her daughter's consent. They both knew it would never be returned, but they didn't mind. Marie often said that the only thing one had to worry about losing was one's honor. What she did mind was the inefficiency and red tape that never formally acknowledged, much less returned, her loan.

The end of the war brought great joy to the Curies. The Armistice meant peace, safety, and rest. Irène received a medal for her war service. For Marie the greatest gift was seeing Poland independent at last, after hundreds of years of oppression. Peace also meant that she could return to the laboratory with a clear conscience. Until 1920, however, the main use of the lab was for the continuation of Irène's radiology course. Chief among her students were some American soldiers who, Marie said approvingly "studied with much zeal."

While Irène taught, Marie wrote. Her *Radiology in War* explained the daring and previously untested ways in which X rays were used during the war. Her contention that both X rays and radium therapy answered a terrible need only enhanced her adoration of science and proved to her that mankind should have confidence, reverence, and admiration for the disinterested research that had provided them.

She also looked for more funds for lab development. Inspired by her war work, she dreamed of establishing an independent hospital and laboratory outside of Paris where scientists would have the space to work together on the enormous quantities of raw materials needed for radioactive research. This new foundation that would bear the Curie name would then be *the* center for radiological studies in the world. Marie did get the money, but in so unexpected a way that her life and career changed dramatically.

After her disastrous bouts with the press in 1911, Marie had refused to have anything more to do with reporters, interviewers, or publicity. Yet in 1920 she succumbed to the request of an American editor named Marie Meloney who was in Europe inspecting the war work her magazine, *The Delineator* (owned by the Butterick pattern company), had sponsored.

Meloney was a high-powered, outgoing organizer with wide-ranging experience. She had met some of the most influential political and social leaders of the day, and felt at home anywhere in the world. When she first approached Marie she had already visited Edison and Bell, and seen that a good scientist could be very wealthy indeed. It is not surprising that she expected a stylishly dressed *"Mother of Radium"* to receive her in an elegant apartment high above the bustle of Paris. How could she not be rich?

On the day of their first meeting Meloney went to the Radium Institute and, in her own words:

> *I waited a few minutes in the small bare office that might have been furnished from Grand Rapids, Michigan. Then the door opened and I saw a pale, timid little woman in a black cotton dress, with the saddest face I had ever looked upon.*
>
> *Her well-formed hands were rough. I noticed a characteristic, nervous little habit of rubbing the tips of her fingers over the pad of her thumb in quick succession. I learned later that working with radium had made them numb. Her kind, patient, beautiful face had the detached expression of a scholar.*

The contrast between the two personalities could not have been greater, yet there was an instant sympathy between them. Part of this attraction was physical; both women were small, delicate, and given to ill health. Their psychological differences only strengthened the bond. Meloney's extroverted enthusiasm was a perfect foil to Marie's introverted quietness. The unexpected friendship that began that day lasted the rest of their lives.

During that first interview, and later in long sessions in Marie's sparsely furnished apartment, Meloney learned the location of each of the fifty grams of radium then in the United States, and that Marie's lab had the only one in France, and that that one was used more for cancer therapy than for research. She learned that the Institute was chronically short of funds and equipment. Cautiously she asked Marie why she was not better provided for and was told proudly that "radium ought not to enrich anyone. It is an element. It belongs to everybody."

Meloney found in these sessions more than dramatic copy about Marie Curie. She found a mission. She proposed to organize a Marie Curie Radium Fund to raise the $100,000 necessary to buy Marie more radium figuring that it wouldn't be very hard to persuade ten wealthy American women to each give $10,000. In return, Marie would have to come to the United States to pick up the radium herself, and Meloney's magazine would get first rights to the story. Although terrified of being in the public eye again, Marie was not averse to a free trip to America and the chance to improve her laboratory.

Meloney could only find three "angels" to put up the money, however. But rather than give up, she shifted gears. Putting her considerable public relations machine to work, she created such a furor that within a year she'd gathered $150,000, almost all of it in small donations. All that was left to do was arrange the trip.

Marie was amazed at the speed and scope of Meloney's work. In weekly cables and letters Marie learned her itinerary, complete with her schedule of lectures and accomodations. Meloney urged her to prepare an autobiography to be promoted during the tour, pointing out that the royalties would provide substantial income for Marie and the lab. By the early spring of 1921 Meloney was able to inform Marie that the President himself would give her the gram of radium (which Meloney had cannily bought from the Soviet Union at half price).

Marie and her daughters sailed for the United States in May, "even though it was not vacation time for me." The French people, finally realizing what a celebrity they had in their midst, gave her a big send-off, complete with a gala performance at the Paris Opera where, among others, an aging Sarah Bernhardt declaimed a poem about radium. A few days later Marie was settled into the bridal suite of the *S.S. Olympic*, her few black gowns hanging in a closet made to hold a trousseau.

The days of the voyage were given to lessons in the language and customs of America, as well as the ins and outs of press conferences. But nothing could have prepared Marie for the scene that greeted her in New York. Tourists, committees, schoolchildren, Girl Scouts, journalists, and three bands playing the French, Polish, and American national anthems all at once, crowded the pier. A frightened Marie stood on the deck surrounded by microphones, cameras, and reporters, and answered a few questions in a small voice before escaping in a borrowed limousine to the silent safety of Meloney's apartment.

The quiet was very temporary. Meloney had arranged such a schedule of scientific meetings, social receptions, lectures, and dinners that Marie could only marvel at the vigor and enthusiasm of her reception. Within a week of her arrival Marie began to bemoan it, too. She took to appearing with her right arm bandaged and in a sling to keep it from being grasped and shaken, and soon began to send Irène and Eve as stand-ins to the events she was too worn out to attend.

Marie visited women's colleges and was pleased with their

Marie's first visit to America was arranged by Marie Meloney (standing). Eve Curie is at her mother's side.

enthusiastic students and rigorous science and physical education courses. Dressed in silken academic robes that irritated her burned fingers, she received honorary degrees from Ivy League schools, despite the vocal protests of conservative male faculty members. She toured hospitals, laboratories, factories, and mines, traveling through Philadelphia, Boston, Washington, and even to the Grand Canyon and Niagara Falls. Everywhere she went she was given gifts of cash, machines, minerals, and sentimental souvenirs.

The gift she had traveled so far to get came on May 20, 1921. The night before, Meloney ran through the ceremony and showed Marie the deed of gift. Marie's eyes were not too tired to notice that the deed gave the radium to her personally, and not to the Institute. She was horrified. She never had and never would own any radium. In the middle of the night she sent Meloney to find a lawyer and a notary to change the deed so that radium could be "consecrated for all time to the use of science." When Meloney suggested gently that this could all be done in the morning, the stubborn scientist replied that she might die before then.

But the next day a very much alive Marie, clad in the same black lace gown she had worn to receive the 1911 Nobel Prize, went to the White House. She listened with pride as President Harding spoke about America's gratitude for Polish help during the Revolution, then thanked him graciously for the symbolic key to the radium's traveling case.

Wearing the same black lace dress in which she had received the Nobel Prize ten years earlier, Marie Curie was presented with a gift of one gram of radium by President Warren G. Harding.

She had her radium, but still was not free to go. Meloney had arranged several more stops for Marie, and other requests kept pouring in. The publicity machine had worked too well. America was so captivated by Marie's love of science, by her indifference to profit, and by her humanitarian spirit, that it would not let her go. The excitement proved too much for Marie in the end, and she began canceling visits and hiding from the press, too exhausted to cope with adoration any longer. An American physicist described meeting her: "I felt sorry for the poor old girl. She was a distinctly pathetic figure. She was very modest and unassuming, and she seemed frightened at all the fuss people made over her."

When Marie finally boarded the *Olympic* for the trip back, she had with her enough money and equipment to outfit her lab as she envisioned. She also had a generous book contract for her autobiography, chemical samples, and radium. Her relationship with Meloney continued to be profitable. Forever after, the energetic editor steered potential patrons to the Curie Pavilion to provide for the Institute's financial health. In gratitude, Marie arranged for Meloney to be awarded France's greatest prize, the Legion of Honor.

After this trip Marie's life changed direction. She now realized, first, that good things come to those who ask and, second, that her presence was a valuable commodity that could help the causes she cared about. During the twenties, Marie moved out of the lab and into the world. She attended meetings and conferences, she traveled, she lectured, and she never came home empty-handed. Her frail appearance and genteel hints opened hearts and purses in Brazil, Holland, Belgium, Italy, England, and Spain.

Other good things came her way. In 1922 she was spontaneously elected to the Academy of Medicine when the other candidates for the seat quit the field and the membership welcomed her to their ranks—the first woman ever to be so honored. And in 1923, on the occasion of the twenty-fifth anniversary of the discovery of radium, the French parliament passed a bill granting the fifty-six-year-old Marie an annual pension that could be inherited by her children. Although honored by the award and touched by the grand ceremony at which it was presented, Marie decided she was too young to give up her work, and so turned the pension into another scholarship for the laboratory.

Marie lent her fame to several causes, the most important being world peace. She served as a member of the Council of the League of Nations, hoping that by promoting understanding among nations another war could be averted. Toward this end she was also busy with the League's International Committee on Intellectual Cooperation. She created an international bibliography of scientific publications, developed a plan for all nations to use standard scientific terms, and set up scholarships to insure that no potential scientist anywhere in the world would have to abandon his or her dream for lack of funds. This Committee also tried to find a fair royalty system so that scientists whose work had been applied freely to society might benefit from their efforts; Marie wanted to spare them her hardships.

But the cause dearest to her heart was the establishment of the Marie Sklodowska-Curie Radium Institute in Warsaw. Since she had organized the lab program there in 1912, Marie had hoped to see it housed in a fine new building, well-equipped with modern apparatus, where her plans could be executed and expanded. In the early 1920s that hope became reality. Spurred by a substantial cash gift from Marie, her sister Bronya tried to organize a building fund à la Meloney. When it became evident that few Poles could afford to be so generous, the practical Bronya started a "Buy-a-Brick" campaign to encourage small donations. She was so successful that by 1925 Marie traveled to Warsaw to lay the cornerstone, and by 1932 she saw it open, staffed, and functioning.

The radium for this lab was once again provided by Marie Meloney. Another large-scale campaign in the United States again netted a surplus of funds for the Polish radium, despite growing economic confusion and an isolationist foreign policy that made Americans wary of giving so much money to a foreign country.

In 1929 a more sophisticated Marie returned to the United States for a tour that, if somewhat quieter than the first, was no less profitable. And it was certainly more enjoyable. A decade of travel had made Marie quite fond of being treated like a queen. In late October President Hoover handed her a check for $50,000 to be used for the radium purchase. From the White House Marie returned to New York, climaxing her visit with a triumphant motorcade down Wall Street to the departing ship.

Three days later that same Wall Street was thronged with panicked investors. The fourth day after Marie had collected her money was Black Thursday, when the stock market crashed and America descended into the Great Depression. The financial cataclysms of the larger world, and the political turmoil they caused, barely touched Marie, however. She had her cash, her equipment, her elements, and her scholarships. She had taken care of what was still most important to her—her laboratory.

PEACE

7

Marie was sixty-seven and she was ill. Fatigue, dizziness, and fever were now her constant companions. As she had done many times before, she acknowledged the symptoms but refused to give in to them, still believing that more rest, or a better diet, or perhaps pure country air would make her better.

But there came a beautiful clear day in May 1934, when she could no longer ignore her uninvited guests. On that afternoon she slowly put down the test tube of actinium she was holding, pushed her chair away from her desk, and whispered to her assistant: "I have a fever. I must go home."

With trembling hands she put on her hat and made her way downstairs. As she waited in the sunlit garden for the chauffeur, Marie noticed that one of the rosebushes was withering, and asked the lab's handyman out for a quick consultation. Her last instructions to the Radium Institute, called from the car as it pulled away from the curb were: "Georges, don't forget that rose. . . ."

humming

blind

Marie had been suffering for years, but had traveled around the world, built labs, and helped the sick, all without telling anyone of her troubles. Since her kidney operation in 1911, she had been plagued by an almost continuous humming in her ears. Sometimes it was so loud that she couldn't follow a conversation. Then, toward the end of the war, an even more alarming symptom developed. Marie began to lose her sight.

At first she thought it was eyestrain that made it so hard for her to read the calibrations on the test tubes. And maybe she just needed to bear down on her pen a little harder so that she could read the figures in her account books. But as her sight kept dimming, Marie resigned herself to blindness, even admitting to her sister Bronya that she didn't think anything could be done to help.

Frightened of becoming helpless, and equally alarmed by the prospect of being treated as a cripple, Marie began to mask her problem. She learned to write her lecture notes in a sprawling hand, and put big brightly colored markers on her lab equipment so that she could easily identify each piece. In order to actually use the electrometers and balances, she had a trusted assistant repaint the dials with heavy black numbers. But the hardest part of her charade was when a student came to discuss a paper, photograph, or chart with her. As there was no way she could decipher it, Marie became a skillful cross-examiner. While she appeared to be studying the document, she asked an endless stream of questions about it, and from that information framed her reply.

No one was fooled of course, but out of the combination of fear and respect she inspired in them, the staff and students at the Institute played along with her act. So did her family. Marie never made a public appearance without one of her daughters to guide her around the room or help her find the forks and spoons at the dinner table. During the first American tour, Marie Meloney took over some of this duty. But Meloney refused to accept Marie's prognosis and took her to an eye specialist. He told her she had cataracts and that if they were removed, Marie would see again.

Marie hesitated for two more years, but by 1923 she was virtually blind. Rather than face a life without work, she agreed to the operation. Still concerned about her privacy, she kept her decision secret even from her daughters until two days before she entered the hospital. Then she swore them to silence, making them promise to tell any curious colleagues that she was just taking a few days off to catch up on some editing.

The operation was long and difficult, but successful. It took three more to get her eyes back to near normal, but after each operation Marie was back in the lab almost as soon as the bandages were off. And with the help of thick glasses, she was soon driving around Paris all by herself.

Marie's frail-looking body disguised an incredible physical toughness that helped her withstand the tremendous stresses she put on herself. After twenty-five years she still kept the same rigorous schedule she had developed in the shed at the School of Physics and Chemistry. Unfortunately, the people she worked with were not as strong as she. During the 1920s Marie heard her colleagues complain of fatigue and aching bones in ever-increasing numbers, and watched some of her students painfully suffer with cancer. Even her good friends Marie Meloney and Loïe Fuller were cancer victims. But what was most upsetting to Marie was the growing suspicion that radium was responsible for all these ailments.

Marie admitted that radium was a dangerous substance, and that "several times I have felt a discomfort which I consider a result of this cause," But she was unwilling to point a finger at her child. "Perhaps radium has something to do with these troubles," she wrote to Bronya about her eyes and ears, "but this cannot be affirmed with certainty." There were others, however, who could be more definite in their opinions.

By the early twenties doctors in large hospitals had recognized a high incidence of cancer deaths among radiologists, X-ray technicians, and their support staffs. Other physicians had documented a tragic coincidence of cancer in women whose war work had been to paint dials and machines with luminous paint. These women had been trained to lick the tips of the paint brushes to get a finer point, and the radium in the paint they ingested from this habit gave them a type of cancer known grimly as "Radium Jaw." Most horrifying, though, were those who had been poisoned by their own medicine. While some cancers showed up right away, even twenty years later doctors were still seeing patients who had liberally dosed themselves with an over-the-counter wonder preparation called "Radiothor" which contained not only radium, but mesothorium as well.

Marie's colleagues, now dying painfully, finally saw the cause, too. They realized how foolish they had been to seek the radium burns that were the proud battle scars and decorations of the Curie laboratory. The radium that marked their skin had hidden in their bones long after the lesions had healed, destroying their blood cells and their resistance, just as Pierre had found in his guinea pigs so many years before. They wept, too late, over their blithe acceptance of Marie's naive prescription for protection from the radiation: she advised new students to change their lab coats frequently, and to take long walks in the country to clear their lungs.

Even Marie came to realize that her humming ears and fogged eyes were all part of the same trouble that had made her and Pierre always so tired. It was radium that had caused his "rheumatism" and her dizziness. She was forced to admit that her discovery, which had done so much good, was also a deadly weapon that could destroy as much as it could cure. But by then the damage had been done. Marie acknowledged radium's culpability and kept on working. Her child may have shortened her life, but she couldn't stop and worry about it.

When Marie wasn't traveling around the world, she lived with her daughters in a big apartment overlooking the River Seine in Paris. The only furniture was what she had inherited from old Dr. Curie; walls, windows, and floors were bare. She and Irène liked living in this uncluttered laboratory-like atmosphere. Only Eve kept trying to personalize the apartment by filling its walls with pictures, its floors with carpets, and its silent halls with the sound of her piano. Marie now kept a chauffeur, maid and cook, but the habit of poverty died hard. Marie herself answered the door so as not to trouble the maid. In the mornings she rushed about the apartment to get ready for work so she wouldn't keep the chauffeur waiting. She still chose the cheapest black dress and the ugliest hat in the shop (Eve often complained that her mother knew nothing of fashion), so as not to spend any more money than absolutely necessary. And, even though she could afford to buy more, the only jewels Marie owned to brighten her grim garments were a gold and garnet necklace, an Indian silver chain she'd purchased at the Grand Canyon, and an old amethyst pin that had belonged to her mother.

Every day Marie went to the Radium Institute. No matter how early she got there, a group of young scientists beginning their careers at her lab would be waiting at the door to greet her with problems and questions about their work. "Why won't this experiment work?" "How can I measure that?" "Please look over this article before I send it off to that journal." Moving slowly down the hall to her office, Marie answered each one in turn with the same impartial tone, agreeing to come observe a procedure or to take a paper home with her for further study. These early morning sessions might last two hours, but Marie never closed her door before the last question had been asked.

How could she? Marie had handpicked all the students at the Institute and assigned their research topics according to their talents. Along with their scholarships came Marie's personal supervision. As her own children grew up, these young scientists took their place in Marie's care. The laboratory became a substitute family, with Marie a stern yet sympathetic mother figure, especially to the young women. Not that she was ever demonstrative. The greatest praise a student could hope for was a quick nod and a terse "Well done." But her pupils knew how important they, and their scientific development, were to the woman they called "La Patronne," even if she never said so.

They recognized the love in her sudden insistence that they wear lead shields to protect themselves against radiation sickness. They appreciated the parties she organized to celebrate the milestones in their careers—a doctorate, a published article, a breakthrough discovery—when they all gathered in a laboratory room or the garden to drink tea out of clean glass beakers, stirring their sugar with glass rods and happily relaxing among the apparatus of the day's work. They understood that the lab was Marie's world, and her teaching and concern showed this second generation of atomic physicists the joys and rewards of a life dedicated to pure science.

Although she was never happier than when she was totally absorbed in an experiment, with all her senses concentrated on the tubes and flasks in front of her and oblivious to the world, Marie was really too busy running the Institute to spend much time in actual research. She had very strong ideas about how to manage the place so that other scientists could study without the worry of finding money or markets for their work, and she trusted no one else to implement them. Marie's ideal was an ivory tower atmosphere enhanced by the endowments and equipment of the giant industrial labs; in other words, modern facilities without any of the commercial pressure she felt "perverted" pure science.

Marie was a great director because she loved the lab, and was a gifted natural teacher who could help all who worked there. One other trait made her successful—perseverance. The skills she had mastered to get her X-ray cars rolling, coupled with her innate singleminded stubborness, helped her hound government agencies, private benefactors, and huge corporations with demands for scholarships, grants, subsidies, and materials. The welfare of her lab was paramount and nothing could stand in her way. When she noticed that the daily rumble of traffic outside the lab was distracting her scientists and disturbing their delicate devices, Marie went straight to the Chief of Police and told him to rearrange Paris' traffic patterns. Within days, one-way streets were reordered, and quiet reigned in the rue Curie.

Another important part of Marie's duties was public relations. Thanks to her own brilliance and Meloney's hard-sell promotion,

Marie Curie had become a household word. Even though most of this celebrity came from the mistaken notion that Marie herself had found a cure for cancer, Marie didn't refute it. Anything that drew attention and aid to the lab had to be cultivated. Marie hired a special secretary who handled the colossal amount of mail coming to the Institute every day by sending a form rejection to requests for autographs and photographs, and filing the rest into one of the forty-seven envelopes in which Marie kept her correspondence.

On Tuesdays and Fridays Marie put on her neatest black dress and received visitors in her office. Interviewers were warned well ahead of time that she would discuss only scientific matters. If a persistent journalist pestered her with personal questions she'd refuse to speak. Marie sat through these ordeals quietly and spoke politely, but remained aloof and distant. Even the most calloused reporter soon noticed the way she rubbed her fingertips and stole glances at the clock on the wall, and would end the appointment early.

If no one needed her in the lab, Marie went home for dinner with her daughters. At the table she and Irène discussed the day's work while Eve wondered what the strange words meant. After dinner Irène usually went back to the lab, and Marie retired to her room to study.

Many times Eve came in late from a date to find her mother still sitting on the floor with her papers, counting to herself in Polish. She would barely acknowledge her daughrer's goodnight kiss. Marie never understood Eve. Her younger daughter was fashionable, sophisticated, and artistic, and had already chosen a journalistic career for herself. But while Marie might disapprove of her child's slinky dresses and red lipstick, she saw that she needed Eve's social contacts and skills to help her cope with the world she had to live in, and she often gave Eve a chance to prove her worth and helpfulness.

Marie had no such problems with Irène. The two had been working together since the war, and after the Armistice Irène had joined the Institute. She was the most brilliant student there and was so obviously following in her mother's footsteps that, when she defended her doctoral dissertation in 1925, Irène faced the same type of crowd of tourists and spectators that had attended Marie's first Sorbonne lecture in 1906.

Irene had inherited more than Marie's aptitudes. She showed the same cavalier attitude toward the harmful effects of radiation and the same persistence in gaining her objectives. A firm believer in the equality of scientific ability in both sexes, Irène still felt that, as science was "the primordial interest in my life," she should "renounce worldly obligations."

But this stern attitude didn't stop her from calmly telling her mother one morning in 1926 that she was going to marry a handsome young physicist from the lab named Frédéric Joliot. Frédéric was so honored to be joining the family that he added Curie to his own last name, a fact about which his mother-in-law was never quite comfortable. Irène and Frédéric proved to be the same brilliant combination of experimentalist and chemist that Marie and Pierre had been and, like the Curies, were always together in the lab.

Marie said that "what I want for women and young girls is a simple family life and some work that will interest them." Irène accomplished both with the birth of her daugher Hélène in 1927. The proud grandmother made a point of meeting the baby every afternoon when the nurse took her to the park. For twenty minutes Marie devoted herself entirely to the child, but when she heard the church bells toll the hour she straightened up, kissed the baby good-bye, and strode off to a meeting or to rejoin the baby's parents in the lab.

Marie's elder daughter, Irène (left), followed her mother's career as a physicist, and the two worked together at the Radium Institute.

For a few weeks out of every summer Marie moved to a little house in the seaside town of L'Arcouest. She had always dreamed of having a country home with its own garden and hedge and singing birds, but she and Pierre had put all their money into their work. Now, in her old age, she had her retreat.

The village was nicknamed "Port Science" because so many of the Sorbonne faculty had homes there, but it was an unwritten law that no one could talk shop. Here Marie found peace and relaxation. She could interrupt her reading with long walks or a swim in the sparkling water. Even quite late in life she boasted about being able to do three hundred yards of breaststroke. Marie enjoyed this demonstration of her physical power, and she was proud of the slim figure her exercise helped her maintain.

Marie was thoroughly enjoying her new roles as Patronne, director, and grandmother, and crowing about how the Joliot-Curies' work was recreating "the fine old days of the lab" when, one day in 1932, she lost her balance and stumbled against a lab desk. Thrusting out her hand to break her fall, she escaped major injury but fractured her wrist.

The arm should have healed easily, but even with the best of care the bones knitted slowly. The accident seemed to have broken Marie's strength as well. Overnight she was an old woman. The buzzing in her ears never left her; she felt dizzy and weak and slightly feverish all the time. She tried her old prescription and took herself off for a vacation in the Alps, but returned to Paris feeling worse than ever.

A few mornings later, Marie awoke with abdominal pains. The doctors examining her recommended the removal of her gall bladder. Marie was more afraid of this than any other medical problem she had ever had because her father had died after a gall bladder operation. Rather than risk his fate, she chose to control her symptoms with proper diet and more rest.

For she couldn't leave the lab yet. Irène and Frédéric were

doing marvelous work with radioisotopes, the radioactive forms of an element. By bombarding aluminum nuclei with radiation, they had created totally new radioactive substances. In essence, the Joliot-Curies showed that they could change one element into another by rearranging its nucleus. The new radioisotopes could then be used in research and medicine just as natural radioelements could, but far more cheaply.

Sadly, not even the excitement of this discovery (for which the Joliot-Curies were to win the Nobel Prize in 1935) could keep Marie going. Feeling mortal for the first time in her life, she wrote long letters to Marie Meloney detailing what was to happen to the radium and the lab after her death. She also went through her files and destroyed all her correspondence, keeping only the love letters from Pierre.

Every day she grew weaker, but more beautiful. A slight fever gave her cheeks a rosy glow; low blood pressure made her skin pale. Suffering made her gaunt and showed off her fine bones. With her white hair and black dress, she was a striking figure, a perfect embodiment of the romantic image of a dedicated scientist.

That May afternoon at the lab Marie knew all her work was done. She never went back to the rue Curie. In fact, she never again left her bed. The doctors said she had bronchitis, then tuberculosis. Traveling under an assumed name to avoid publicity, Eve took her mother to a sanatorium in the mountains where Marie could convalesce in clean air and quiet.

The doctors there recognized her illness for what it was— pernicious anemia caused by radium poisioning. The rays that could save lives when used carefully were taking the life of their discoverer. By now, Marie was too weak to hold a thermometer or record her daily temperature in her account book.

It was Eve, her "other daughter," who took care of her until the end. To spare her mother the anguish of knowing she was dying, Eve chose not to tell Marie the diagnosis. She also forbade any last-ditch treatments or last-minute family reunions so that Marie wouldn't be alarmed. Eve sat with her, nursed her, read to her from books and letters. One of the last letters Marie got was from Jacques Curie. As he had done for almost forty years, he admonished her to take better care of herself.

On a day in early July, Marie started feeling better. Her temperature dropped, and she peacefully gazed out the windows and thanked the mountain air for her recovery. That night she began to babble and speak to ghosts; her last clear words were: "I want to be let alone." At dawn on July 4, 1934, the badly burned fingers that had done so much stopped their nervous movement forever.

The funeral was simple and quiet. She was buried with the things she loved in the little cemetery at Sceaux. As her coffin was lowered into Pierre's grave, Joseph and Bronya stepped forward from the tiny knot of mourners and covered their little sister's casket with rich handfuls of Polish earth.

Marie Curie lived to see the world she'd dreamed of as a youth, a world where science sought and found the answers to mankind's problems. Laboratories became the temples of the twentieth century, and scientists the priests who toiled to find new ways to heal the sick, feed the hungry, and clothe the naked.

Radium has helped them improve the world, too, and in ways Marie could not have imagined on that spring night in 1898 when she knew she'd found her treasure at last. Geologists now use radium to determine the age of the earth and its crust by applying Pierre's exponential law of decay to mineral samples and fossils. Industrialists mix radium with phosphorescent chemicals that glow when struck by its rays, and the luminous paint they produce has allowed us to read in the dark. Penetrating radiation finds cracks in heavy machinery and airplanes, and measures the thickness of metal pipes. The rays also preserve and sterilize food. But the element is most famous for its role in cancer diagnosis and treatment. Although radioisotopes are now taking over the job, it was Marie's discovery that pioneered a therapy that alleviated suffering and brought hope to millions of people.

Radium has proven to be a mixed blessing, however. We know now that it can cause cancer and that the symptoms of radiation sickness are many and varied. And other scientists, insatiably curious about the source of radiation, embarked on research that led them to discover fission—the splitting of an atom by bombarding it with alpha rays. Fission produces a tremendous amount of energy, energy which can run engines, submarines, and power plants. But we now have a problem with disposing of the dangerous radioactive waste products from these reactors. Fission has also given us the means to destroy ourselves, because it is the principle of the atomic bomb.

The radium that made Marie famous is not her greatest achievement. Her real impact came with that brilliant hypothesis upon which she based all of her life's work: that radioactivity is the result of something happening within the atom itself. Her simple statement spurred other scientists to study the complexity of atomic structure, to seek the solution to the mysterious behavior of the radioelements that Marie exposed in her experiments. No longer do we see matter as unchanging, impregnable, or inanimate; no longer is the atom a tiny ball, but a miniature solar system full of more particles and forces than the physics of Marie's childhood could ever have envisioned. This tiny woman with her decigram of radium turned the world upside down, forever changing the way we look at, understand, and use our environment.

But in her time, Marie could never have been the first woman to make a significant contribution to science without undergoing constant struggle and sacrifice. In order to be taken seriously by the male scientific establishment, she had to prove herself more than their equal, to work twice as hard and thrice as carefully, to hide her sensitive nature behind a wall of privacy, to deny the joys and obligations of children and home.

Marie Curie was willing to do this for the satisfaction of dedicating her life to science. She consecrated herself to research as a nun commits herself to God—with determination, courage, and zeal. Her vocation affected her body as well as her soul. Paul Appell, her teacher, once described her as "nothing more than a flame." Half a century after her death, Marie Curie's inspiration, strength, and spirit continue to light the world.

FOR FURTHER READING

*Bigland, Eileen. *Madame Curie*. New York: S.G. Phillip's, 1957.

*Curie, Eve. *Madame Curie*. New York: Doubleday, 1938.

Curie, Marie. *Pierre Curie: With Autobiographical Notes*. New York: Dover, 1963 (reproduction ed. of 1927 Macmillan book).

McKown, Robin. *Marie Curie*. New York: Putnam, 1971.

Reid, Robert. *Marie Curie*. New York: Dutton, 1974.

*Suitable for younger readers.

INDEX

Page numbers in italics refer to illustrations.

Academy of Medicine, 98–99
Academy of Science, 41, 57, 78–79
Achievements of Marie Curie, summarized, 115
Alexandrovitch Scholarship, 25–26
Alpha rays, 45, 46, 55, 115
Appell, Paul, 20, 70, 116
Atom, historical concept of, 37, 55; structure of, 40, 56, 115
Atomic bomb, 115
Atomic physics, 37, 56
Autobiography, 90, 93, 98

Barium, 42, 47
Becquerel, Henri, 38–39
Bernhardt, Sarah, 94
Beta rays, 46
Bohr, Niels, 56
Cancer, 105–06, 109, 115; therapy, 53, 93, 114–15
Carnegie, Andrew, 73
Collaboration of Marie and Pierre, 41–47, 52–59, 60
Comte, Auguste, 11
Curie, Dr. (Pierre's father), 70, 76
Curie, Eve Denise (daughter), 63, 74, 76, 94, 95; education of, 75;
and Marie, 76, 104, 106, 109, 113–14
Curie, Irène. *See* Joliot-Curie
Curie, Jacques (Pierre's brother), 70, 71, 114
Curie, Marie (née Sklodowska), appearance of, 10, 15, 16, 28, 92, 107, 111, 113; birth of, 3; childhood of, 3–7; children of, *see* Curie, Eve; Joliot-Curie, Irène; courtship of, 29–30; death of, 114; education of, 7–11, 13–14, 19–25, 24, 26, 36, 52; as governess, 12–14; health of, 8, 58, 78, 80, 92, 103, 112–14, (*see also* Radiation sickness); home life of, 33–35, 59, 106–07; marriage of, 30; meeting Pierre, 26–27; as mother, 35, 63, 73–77; parents of, 3–5, 14, 57; study habits of, 6, 13–14, 21–24; widowed, 70–72. *See also* Collaboration; Honors; Laboratories; Teaching
Curie, Maurice (nephew), 73
Curie Pavilion. *See* Radium Institute
Curie, Pierre, appearance and personality of, 28, 60, 69; courtship of, 29–30; death of, 70; early achievements of, 27–28; education of, 27, 29, 57; health of, 46, 57–58, 67–68; laboratory, 39–40, 42–43, 43, 59, 67; marriage

of, 30; and profit from research, 28, 54. *See also* Collaboration; Honors; Teaching
Curie point, 28
Curie unit of radiation, 78
Curie's Law, 28

Darwin, Charles, 11, 36
Debierne, André, 45
Demarçay, Eugène, 51, 53
Diary, Marie's, 70–71
Dluska, Bronya S. (sister), 3, 8, 9, *10*, 12, *15*, 19–21, 29, 30, 71, 114; letters to, 45, 58, 105; and tuberculosis hospital, 63
Dluski, Casimir, 19–21, 29, 30

Electrometer, 27, 39, 40
Electroscope, 14, 40
Feminism, 12, 72. *See also* Women
Fission, 115
Floating university, 9–11, 13
Fuller, Loïe, 62

Gamma rays, 46
Gymnasium, Marie's, 7–8

Harding, Warren G., 93, *96*, 97
Honors, prizes, and gifts, 25–26, 57, 59, 62–64, 73, 80, 93–97, 98–99, 100
Hoover, Herbert, 100

International scientific work, 99

Joliot-Curie, Frédéric (son-in-law), 110; and radioisotopes, 112–13
Joliot-Curie, Hélène (grandchild), 110
Joliot-Curie, Irène (daughter), 35, *74*, 76, 94, *111*; education of, 75, 110; and Marie, 76, 104, 109-10; marriage of, 110; scientific career of, 91, 110-13; in World War I, 88-90

Kapital, Das (Marx), 13

Laboratories, 14; at School of Physics and Chemistry, 39–40, 42–44, *43*, 67, 86; at the Sorbonne, *24*, 67, 68, 71, 72, 73, *see also* Radium Institute; in Warsaw, 85-99
Laboratory conditions, poor, 41, 42–44, 51–52
Langevin, Paul, 79–80
L'Arcouest, France, 112
Lead, as radiation shield, 53, 107
League of Nations, 99
Legion of Honor, 57, 98

Madame Curie (biography by Eve), 76
Marie Curie Radium Fund, 93
Marie Sklodowska-Curie Radium Institute (Warsaw), 85, 99–100
Marx, Karl, 13
Mathematics, master's degree in, 25–26
Meloney, Marie, 92–98, *95*, 100, 104, 105, 108, 113
Mendeleyev, Dmitri, 37

Nobel Prize in chemistry, 80
Nobel Prize in physics, 59, 62–64; awarded to the Joliot-Curies, 113

Paris, 19–21; as Marie's goal, 9-16; student days in, 19–25; in World War I, 86-87, 90
Pasteur, Louis, 11, 36, 61
Pension for Curie family, 99
Physics, 37, 55; doctorate in, 36, 52; master's degree in, 20; nuclear, 37, 56, 115
Piezoelectricity, 27, 39, 40
Pitchblende, 41, 42–45, 46
Planck, Max, 56
Poland, independence of, 91; Marie's love of, 6, 7, 11, 13, 26; trips

to, 25–26, 85; Russification of, 5–6, 7, 9–10, 85. *See also* Floating university
Polonium, 42, 44, 55, 77
Positivism, 11–12, 78
Poverty, 5, 6, 9, 22–23, 42, 45–46, 56–57
Press, the, 61, 72, 79–81, 92–94, 98

Radiation, nature of, 40, 45–46, 56
Radiation sickness, 46, 57–58, 67–68, 105–06, 107–08, 113–14
Radioactive wastes, 115
Radioactivity, cause of, 115; named, 40; in pitchblende, 41–42; search for, 39–47, 51–52; teaching, 77
Radioelements, and Curie method, 40, 41–42, 45, 55, 115
Radioisotopes, 112–13, 115
"Radiologic car," 88–90
Radiology in War (Marie Curie), 91
"Radiothor," 106
Radium, 42; atomic weight of, 47, 51, 77; as cancer-causing element, 105–06, 114; gifts of, 97, 100; impact of, on scientists, 55–56; isolating, 41, 42–44, 45, 46–47, 51–52, 77, 80; medical uses of, 53, 90, 91, 93; properties of, 51, 52–53, 55; public interest in, 61–62; uses of, summarized, 114–15
Radium burns, 46, 53, 92
Radium chloride, 51, 77
Radium industry, 53, 54
Radium Institute (France), 85–86, 92, 98, 103, 104, 107–09, 110, 111; X-ray training at, 89–90
Religious views, Marie's, 5, 12, 75
Research methods, 46
Röntgen, Wilhelm, 37–38, 39
Rutherford, Ernest, 55–56, 78

Sceaux, France, 30, 70, 76

School of Physics and Chemistry, Paris, 26, 39–40, 42–44, *43*, 45, 67, 86
Sklodowska, Bronya.
  See Dluska
Sklodowska, Hela (sister), 3, 15, 30
Sklodowska, Madame (mother), 3, 4–5
Sklodowska, Marie.
  See Curie, Marie
Sklodowska, Zosia (sister), 3, 5
Sklodowski, Joseph (brother), 3, 8, 23, 114
Sklodowski, Vladislav (father), 3–4, 5–6, 14, *15*, 30, 57
Soddy, Frederick, 55
Sorbonne, the, 20–21; laboratory at, *24*, 67, 68, 71, 72, 73; Marie studying at, 19–25, *24*, 26, 36; Marie teaching at, 72–73, 77; Pierre teaching at, 67. *See also* Radium Institute
Spectroscope, 51

Teaching (by Marie), 13, 29, 34, 35; at the Radium Institute, 107–08; at Sèvres, 45, 57, 67; at the Sorbonne, 72–73; (by Pierre), 26, 45, 67
Thorium, 40, 41, 55
Treatise on Radioactivity (Marie Curie), 78

United States tours, 94–98, *95*, *96*, 100
Uranium, 38–39, 40, 41, 42, 44

Women, prejudice against, 8–9, 36, 72–73, 78–79, 115; as wartime X-ray operators, 89–90
Works of Pierre Curie, 77
World War I, 86–91

X rays, 37–38, 87–90, 91

J   Manor c.2
BIOG.
CURIE
Keller
  MARIE CURIE